AF352615

MEDUSA'S EAR

MEDUSA'S EAR

University Foundings from Kant to *Chora L*

DAWNE MCCANCE

STATE UNIVERSITY OF NEW YORK PRESS

The Head of Medusa, Alinari Art Resource, New York; Uffizi, Florence, Italy.
Self-Portrait with Bandaged Ear, Courtauld Institute of Art, London.
Draughtsman Drawing a Nude in Perspective, Foto Marburg / Art Resource, New York.
A Pair of Shoes, 1887, The Baltimore Museum of Art, Maryland.
My Shoe is Your Shoe, The Andy Warhol Foundation for the Visual Arts / ARS, New York.
Untitled (Shoe and Leg), The Andy Warhol Foundation for the Visual Arts / ARS, New York.
Diamond Dust Shoes, The Andy Warhol Foundation for the Visual Arts / ARS, New York.
Diamond Dust Shoes, hung upside down, The Andy Warhol Foundation for the Visual Arts / ARS, New York.
A Pair of Shoes, F 255, Amsterdam, van Gogh Museum (Vincent van Gogh Foundation).
Nunotani Corporation Headquarters Building. Eisenman, architects. Shigeo Ogawa/Shinkenchiku.
Parc de la Villette. Bernard Tschumi, architects / J. M. Monthiers.
Exploding *Folie*. Bernard Tschumi, architects.
La Villette. Eisenman Robertson, architects. Canadian Center for Architecture, Montréal, Québec.

Published by
STATE UNIVERSITY OF NEW YORK PRESS, ALBANY

© 2004 State University of New York

All rights reserved

Printed in the United States of America

No part of this book may be used or reproduced in any manner whatsoever without written permission. No part of this book may be stored in a retrieval system or transmitted in any form or by any means including electronic, electrostatic, magnetic tape, mechanical, photocopying, recording, or otherwise without the prior permission in writing of the publisher.

For information, address the State University of New York Press, 90 State Street, Suite 700, Albany, NY 12207

Production, Laurie Searl
Marketing, Michael Campochiaro

Library of Congress Cataloging-in-Publication Data

McCance, Dawne, date.
    Medusa's ear : university foundings from Kant to *Chora L* / Dawne McCance.
      p. cm.
    Includes bibliographical references (p.) and index.
    ISBN 0-7914-6247-1 (alk. paper)
    1. Education, Higher—Philosophy. 2. Philosophy, European. 3. Postmodernism and higher education. 4. Derrida, Jacques. I. Title.

LB2322.2.M33 2004
378'.001—dc22
                                        2003069330

10 9 8 7 6 5 4 3 2 1

for Robert, and

for Carson, Patrick, Erin, and Rob

Viviparous quadrupeds utter voiced sounds of different kinds, but they have no language. In fact, this is peculiar to man. For while whatever has language has voice, not everything that has voice has language. Men that are born deaf are in all cases also dumb; that is, they can make vocal sounds, but they cannot speak.

—Aristotle, *History of Animals*

Can we use the senses vicariously? that is, can we use one sense as a substitute for another? If a deaf man was once able to hear, we can get him to speak as he used to by gesturing to him, and so by means of his eyes. He can also use his eyes to read our lips, or his sense of touch to feel our lip movements in the dark. If, however, he has been deaf from birth, his sense of *sight* must begin with movements of the vocal organs and convert the sounds he has been taught to make into a feeling of moving the muscles of his own vocal organs. But he never arrives at real concepts in this way, because the signs he uses are not the sort that can be universalized.

—Kant, *Anthropology from a Pragmatic Point of View*

In textbooks, images of developing embryos look like the outer shell of the ear. And our ability to hear is the first sense to develop in utero and the last to shut down before death. With infinite divisibility, sound is decoded in the remotest reaches of the inner ear. Deep inside the auricular labyrinth—the oracle—there are microscopic bones called ossicles which are said to resemble the bones of our feet. The last extreme of littleness, Edmund Burke wrote, is in some measure sublime.

—Evelyn Juers, "She Wanders"

CONTENTS

ILLUSTRATIONS

ACKNOWLEDGMENTS

I wish to acknowledge the support I received for researching and writing this book from the Social Sciences and Humanities Research Council of Canada. I also want to acknowledge the Markin-Flanagan Writer-in-Residence program at the University of Calgary; the Office of the Dean, Faculty of Arts, and the Office of the Vice-President, Research, at the University of Manitoba; Melanie Lewis; my students; and Jane Bunker, Laurie Searl, and the publishing team at SUNY Press.

ABBREVIATIONS

CM   "Canons and Metonymies: An Interview With Jacques Derrida"

CW   *Chora L Works* (with Peter Eisenman)

DO   "Deconstruction and the Other: An Interview with Richard Kearney"

EO   *The Ear of the Other: Otobiography, Transference, Translation*

G   *Glas* (my page references follow the system used by John Leavey's *Glassary*, with *a* and *b* denoting the left- and right-hand columns of the text, and with *i* denoting the inserts in both columns)

G1   "*Geschlecht*: sexual difference, ontological difference"

GII   "*Geschlecht* II: Heidegger's Hand"

GIV   "Heidegger's Ear: Philopolemology (*Geschlecht* IV)"

GD   *The Gift of Death*

HAS   "How to Avoid Speaking: Denials"

LIP   "Languages and Institutions of Philosophy."

M   "*Mochlos*; or, The Conflict of the Faculties"

MB   *Memoirs of the Blind: The Self-Portrait and Other Ruins*

MP   *Margins of Philosophy*

OAT   "Of an Apocalyptic Tone Recently Adopted in Philosophy"

OCP   "On Colleges and Philosophy"

OG   *Of Grammatology*

OH   *The Other Heading: Reflections on Today's Europe*

OHS   *Of Hospitality: Anne Dufourmantelle Invites Jacques Derrida to Respond*

OS   *Of Spirit: Heidegger and the Question*

P   *Positions*

Pf   *"Point de folie: Maintenant l'architecture"*

PR   "The Principle of Reason: The University in the Eyes of its Pupils"

PT   *Points . . . Interviews 1974–1994*

R   *Resistances of Psychoanalysis*

RM   "The *Retrait* of Metaphor"

SA   "The Spatial Arts: An Interview with Jacques Derrida"

SM   *Specters of Marx*

SP   *Speech and Phenomena and Other Essays on Husserl's Theory of Signs*

TP   *The Truth in Painting*

WD   *Writing and Difference*

ONE

MOURNING THE VOICE

Deaf and dumb go hand in hand.

—Derrida, Speech and Phenomena

OS(SIS) MUTUM

IT'S THE TERRIFYING ASPECT of the mortal Gorgon that Caravaggio captures in his *Medusa's Head*, the image a reminder of just how dangerous it can be to look. In mythology, the mere sight of this snake-tressed monster would turn a man to stone; to see her face is to die. And according to Mieke Bal, Caravaggio's painting portrays Medusa as just this *femme fatale*, "a representative of the killing powers attributed to women by men" in the culture that is "ours, today's" (Bal 1996, 57). The killing powers of women derive from a male fantasy of loss: Freud explains in his 1940 essay on Medusa that when a man looks at the monster's decapitated head, he sees a woman's genitals, and becomes stiff (erect) with the terror of his own castration (Freud [1940] 1953, 273). For Bal, however, this story—which ties loss to vision and which constructs the viewing subject as male—is made for the modern age and for the culture that is "ours, today's" for the reason that, to use her words, "although Medusa allegedly killed by means of looking, she ended up dead by being looked at" (Bal 1996, 9). This is the model of vision on which modern discursivity is supposedly based. What Hal Foster (1988, x) calls "Cartesian perspectivalism" separates the always-male viewing subject from the feared object of his gaze, so that the subject is made transcendental

1

Perseus cried, "Friends, shield your eyes!" and with Medusa's face, he changed
the king's face to a bloodless stone.

Ovid, *Metamorphoses*

Figure 1. *The Head of Medusa*, oil on canvas, mounted on a wooden shield, by
Michelangelo Merisi da Caravaggio, 1590–1600. Galleria Uffizi, Florence, Italy.

and so that the othered-object—the body, the woman—is reified and
left dead.

Critics take the emergence of this model of vision to be deter-
minative of the shift from medieval to modern. Erwin Panofsky explains that to a Renaissance theoretician such as Albrecht Dürer (whose
1527 woodcut *Draughtsman Drawing a Nude* I discuss in chapter 5),
perspective in the visual arts was a new way of "seeing through" the

material surface of the picture or painting from the centric point of a so-called visual pyramid. The eye that looked from the apex of this pyramid through the transparent "window" of the canvas was considered to be single, lone, and immobile, set entirely apart from what it perceived to be a linear and mathematical world (Panofsky 1991, 27–36). The lone eye was also considered to be singular, vehicle of the "clear and distinct" knowledge of Cartesian rational philosophy. Descartes' philosophy disembodied the all-seeing *res cogito*, claiming certainty for the spectator by cutting vision off from all affect.[1] It banished what Martin Jay calls the "moment of erotic projection in vision—what Augustine had anxiously condemned as 'ocular desire,'" as the bodies of viewing subject and viewed object were "forgotten in the name of an allegedly disincarnated, absolute eye" (Jay 1988, 8). And although the gaze could still fall on an object of desire—as when Dürer's draughtsman, sitting stiffly erect and a safe distance removed, looks through a screen of perspectival threads and eyes the prostrate female nude—it did so by way of a Medusa-like petrification, "a reifying male look that turned its targets into stone" (8).

In traditional Medusa mythology and iconography, "it is crucial that the killing happen by visual means" (Bal 1996, 57): the monster is slain for her looks and her effect—the Medusa effect—in turn, is to kill men for looking at her. As such a figure of the power of sight, and of the reifying potential of Cartesian vision, Medusa is often drawn into critical analyses of modernity as an ocularcentric regime, the transition to which is claimed to involve displacement of the ear by the perspectival eye. The story of the eye's hegemony in modernity, "the sovereign nobility of vision, ostensibly redoubled by the Enlightenment," is one of the dominating narratives of contemporary critical theory, Leigh Eric Schmidt, I think rightly, maintains (Schmidt 2000, 7). The grand narrative is not one I subscribe to in this book. Indeed, in this and subsequent chapters, I take issue with the assumption that modernity is centered solely on (a single model of) vision and that it involves "the eye's clear eclipse of the ear" (15).[2] At the same time, ocularcentrism is a narrative with which I must consistently contend, and for the reason that it makes modernity the story of a profound *hearing loss*. Such is the fantasy of loss that interests me in this book, where I track the trope—and terror—of the always-gendered deaf ear in the discourse on the university that is inaugurated by Kant's *The Conflict of the Faculties* and that extends through Hegel and Heidegger to the present. In the readings I undertake in this book, it's the fantasy of the lost ear, and by extension the lost tongue, that I foreground and put into question. What draws me to Caravaggio's Medusa, then, is her fully open mouth: terrifying and terrified, at once silent and caught in a death scream, Medusa's mouth, Bal suggests, "fulfills its traditional function as a symbol of the vagina dentata which, as an exteriorized projection of castration anxiety, petrifies the enemy" (Bal 1991, 320–21). I propose that Medusa's mouth petrifies as the sign of a woman struck deaf, and therefore, dumb. In support of the proposition, this book's next three chapters find that, over and over again, in foundational texts on the modern research university, the philosopher-subject recoils in fear from an othered-object (body, woman) he defines as deaf and mute. This withdrawal has the effect—the Medusa effect—of cutting off the philosopher's, and therefore the institution's, own ear and tongue. According to my reading of this Medusa effect, the modern university is petrified. It needs to be shaken—solicited—into movement, a matter I explore in the last two chapters of the book.

What I see in the Caravaggio painting, as prefiguring my task in this book, is not a woman temporarily dumbfounded, but incapable of speech, altogether mute; a woman who, like Philomela, has had her tongue cut off. It's this silent Medusa, this icon of speechlessness, that Lynn Enterline takes from the *Metamorphoses*, the Medusa who, throughout Ovid's poem, utters not a single word. Thanks to Freud's 1940 essay, we think of the Medusa effect "predominantly in terms of a visual trauma," Enterline writes. "But in Ovid's text it is not Medusa's 'head,' or even her gaze, that petrifies. Rather, it is primarily her silenced 'face' or 'mouth' (*os, oris*)" (Enterline 2000, 16). Charles Segal notes that the name Gorgon comes from "the Indo-European root *garj*, denoting a fearful shriek, roar, or shout" (Segal 1994a, 18; qtd. in Enterline 2000, 17). Drawing on a long tradition that associates the Gorgon with disturbing oral fantasies, Ovid singles out Medusa's *os* as, Enterline says, in the first place, a disabled or mute mouth, a "face deprived of the capacity to speak" (Enterline 16). This silent *os* is, in turn, the instrument of petrification. "[B]ecause they confront Medusa's terrifying mouth (*os*), numerous male victims stand forever petrified by the force of this *monstrum*" (28).

According to modern ocularcentrism, the narrative with which I try to reckon in this book, Western culture still holds on to the voice as the very essence of identity, the "vibrant principle" of life itself (Rée 1999, 3),[3] and for this reason, although some distance removed from Ovid, modernity's subject remains haunted by the fear of an *os mutum*, the fantasy of a mouth that cannot speak and of a voice that has been lost. In the theorizing of the medieval-to-modern transition as the passage from orality to a resolutely perspectival regime, the fear of the *os mutum* would seem to be realized.[4] And indeed, while some critics concede that different modes of looking developed in the modern era, few question the dominance of the detached spectatorial model, this model as what enabled a new technological science and an individualist social physics, as what turned vision into modernity's master sense, and as what marked the historic defeat of a vocal and auditory culture, one attuned by its ear to the voice. So contends Jonathan Rée, citing Oswald Spengler:

> The "thought of the eye," as Spengler called it, gave birth to a proud, solitary and resolute subjectivity, cynically surveying the abstract light-world that surrounds it. The optical mind was the master of mechanical invention, but too fascinated by "static, optical details" to have any sense of the tragedy and mystery of "life." Vision had cut us off from the ancient wisdom of ordinary pre-theoretical mutuality, annihilating vocality and, with it, the "inward kinship of I and Thou." Now that modern civilization was confronting its ultimate crisis—a crisis of its own making, a crisis of technology—it was stumbling uncomprehendingly towards catastrophe: twentieth-century humanity, Spengler thought, having lost its voice and its sense of hearing, was destined to "go downhill *seeing*". (Rée 1999, 4)

Modernity's promotion of sight as what Descartes (in the *Optics*) called "the noblest and most comprehensive of the senses" (Descartes 1985, 152) is thus claimed to be the beginning of the end of the voice. It is important to note that in this account, loss of the voice is also a loss of hearing, an attenuation of the sense that is said to have surpassed all others in significance in the earlier oral and manuscript culture for which communication of knowledge depended on speech. In an oral culture, Donald Lowe explains, adopting the thesis of Walter Ong, communication is aural and "speech has to be heard proximately and instantly, since there is no telephone, phonograph, radio, or audiotape and disc to relay a spoken message across space or time. Speech is assimilated directly by the ear, without the mediation of the eye. And we are moved more by sound than by sight, since the former surrounds us, whereas the latter distances" (Lowe 1982, 7). With the transition from medieval oral and chirographic culture to modern typography, visuality overthrows aural immediacy, as Lowe tells the familiar story; communication now takes place by reading, "the silent assimilation of the message by the eye" (8). The philosophers of modernity whom Rée calls "friends of the voice" are, he says, as anxious about this displacement of the auditory as they are about the annihilation of speech. Their anxiety is fed by Heidegger's "doleful ruminations" about the consequences, for Western culture, of its shift to an age where the world becomes "picture" (Rée 1999, 5).

Inasmuch as this ocularcentric narrative of loss concerns both speech and hearing, the figure that it finds most frightening must be not only dumb but also deaf. Certainly, these two, "deaf and dumb," have always been put together in the Western tradition; the deaf ear as counterpart of the mute mouth, the mouth that, as Aristotle explained, is *speechless*, though it can emit animal sounds. In a tradition for which, as Rée suggests, even minor speech impediments such as stammering or lisping constitute "an appalling spiritual [and mental] calamity" (Rée 1999, 89), mutism is deemed equivalent to the death of the mind or *animus*. Even more catastrophic is prelingual deafness for the reason that, as I make the case in this book, it constitutes a more originary lack: in this tradition, one is considered dumb, in every sense of the word, *because* one is deaf—that is, not only lacking speech, but also the sound-concept identity that philosophers of modernity consider essential to self-presence. Deafness confers a primordial nonplenitude; from the start, we might say, it locates one outside of ideal immediacy, in the mundane, mobile register of division and delay that Derrida associates with *différance*. Perhaps this is the reason why the Western literary tradition offers no stories of "noble" deaf mutes. "Literary dumbness, it seems, afflicts victims rather than heroes, others rather than self, females rather than males" (91–92). This is in marked contrast to the rich literature the tradition provides on blindness, for instance the many stories of "great blind men" (MB 5) that Derrida takes up in his *Memoirs of the Blind*—"great, paradigmatic narratives of blindness" that are dominated "by the filiation father/son" (5–6, n1), and that make male blindness a condition of extraordinary insight. We have no deaf and dumb sages to set alongside these blind seers. Given that the voice in this tradition is, as seventeenth-century thinker Francis Mercury van Helmont contended, "an expression of male sexual strength" (qtd. in Rée 1999, 3), muteness, death of the *animus*, is a castration of the principle of sexual prowess. There can be no father/son filiation where the virile voice has been cut off. Nor can there even be successful femininity where the ear, as deaf, is blocked to reception of the male's inseminating speech.

The terrifying, disabled, *os* that I see in Caravaggio's Medusa is a *monstrum* that I want to translate in these dual terms, as evoking both oral and aural trauma, both a mute mouth and, even prior to that, a deaf ear. I argue in this book that the two, mute mouth and deaf ear, belong inseparably—as "other"—to the fantasy that Derrida calls *phonocentric*. To say this is to challenge the conventional reading of phonocentrism as solely about the hierarchy of speech/writing, about the Western prejudice for *speaking*, for the voice, as, in conjunction with light-sight, the *eye*, the essence of the rational-spiritual self. I suggest that, even more than speech, phonocentrism privileges hearing. Notwithstanding the story of the ear's eclipse, and no doubt supporting this fantasy of loss, phonocentrism builds on an *audiocentric* imaginary, one for which the trauma of speechlessness comes second, as it were, to the fear of loss or lack of hearing.[5] To bypass hearing—as critical analyses of phonocentrism commonly do, with their focus on speech and on the contest between speaking and writing—is to miss the anxiety that deafness provokes in the Western tradition, where, associated with dumbness, darkness, and death, its powers are, to say the least, killing. As I demonstrate in the following pages, audiocentrism does not diminish the importance accorded to light and sight in this tradition: indeed, the coming out of darkness to light is, Derrida says, the founding metaphor of Western philosophy as metaphysics (WD 27). The metaphor is at once spatial and temporal: as in Hegel, it gives the story of beginnings and of the ascending East-to-West journey of spirit through historical time, which is also an account of the sun's, spirit's, interiorizing *return-to-itself*. Western metaphysics is so bound up with the narrative of its coming to light out of darkness that the entire history of our philosophy could be considered a "photology," Derrida suggests, "a history of, or treatise on, light" (27). This photology posits an immediate relationship between the voice and the light-sight (*theoria*, *eidos*, clarity, visibility, revelation, intelligibility, *telos*, etc.) of the mind—and precisely in so doing, as critics have not sufficiently noted, it joins speech and sight to the ear, all fully interiorized and ideal. Within the mind of the phonocentric imaginary, phonetic sound, a word, is *heard* "first," and as "heard," is what enables a metaphysical idea, a concept, to be made present, visible, to the self. "*Phonè*, in effect, is the signifying substance *given to consciousness* as that which is most intimately tied to the thought of the signified concept" (P 22). In metaphysics, Derrida maintains, this "original and essential link to the *phonè* has never been broken" (OG 11).

Since, as Oliver Sacks points out, the prelingually deaf "have no auditory image, no *idea* of what speech actually sounds like, no idea of a sound-meaning correspondence" (Sacks 1989, 26), and thus no phonetic inwardness to start with, they must represent a terrifying otherness for the phonocentric imaginary. The prelingually deaf are lacking the voice that, as in the case of Husserl, brings to light for consciousness the ideal being of an object present before its gaze, the voice that, as Derrida puts it in chapter 6 of *Speech and Phenomena*, "keeps silent" because it is heard *before* it is materialized as speech. Of course, the prelingually deaf are speechless; they have their tongues cut off, and so must resort to what Aristotle considered to be "animal aping" (see MP 237). It is important to note, however, that, within a phonocentric fantasy, the spoken word serves as but a medium of the "interior voice," with writing, one step further removed, "as mediation of mediation and as fall into the exteriority of meaning" (OG 12–13). What is fascinating and frightening about muteness, then, is the interior lack that it supposedly reveals: the prelingually deaf cannot speak *because they have no inner ear*; they are without access to the interiority through which "I hear myself [*je m'entendre*] *at the same time that I speak*" (SP 77). Derrida refers to this idealized speaking-hearing simultaneity as *hearing-oneself-speak*; the term is one I will resort to several times in this book. On one level, I will use the term *hearing-oneself-speak* to denote phonocentrism's idealization of the ear: its disengagement of hearing from all exteriority, from "facial expressions, gestures, the whole of the body and the mundane register, in a word, the whole of the visible and the spatial as such" (35). Even the postlingually deaf are outside of the ideal of *hearing-oneself-speak*, for they, too, lack the plenitude of an inner speech that can be "heard" independently of lip reading, writing, hand signing, or some other props or prostheses. As well, they are caught up from the start in the sort of linguistic spacing that phonocentrism attempts to collapse.[6] In a phonocentric culture, then, they belong on the other side of the us/ them line. This is the second level on which I will use the term *hearing-oneself-speak*, as a designator of phonocentrism's inevitable collusion with hierarchical—sexist, racist, and colonialist—political structures.

LABYRINTH

That Western culture's fantasy of the lost voice, the fantasy Derrida calls phonocentric, builds on a dual—oral and aural—trauma is, I have suggested, a point that is not often made; typically, accounts of phonocentrism attend only to the mouth and to speech. Lynn Enterline's *The Rhetoric of the Body* is a case in point. In this study, Enterline notes that the Latin noun, *os* (*oris*), which is at the root of the English "oracular," is difficult to render as one word. Ovid's narrator "constantly reminds us of its etymological resonances, tracing a tropological sequence with rich cultural significance for his thinking about poetic voice and for some of our most deeply ingrained ideas about language and persons" (Enterline 2000, 16). Yet, for all the etymological surplus Enterline uncovers in the word—including "the mouth as an organ of speech," "the lips," "the voice," "the mouth of a poet," "the face," "the features," "expression," "gaze," "mood," and "character"—she makes no mention of the ear, and this in a study of the disabled *os* that extends from Ovid to Shakespeare (16).[7] In the following pages, I will be concerned with the *os* (*ossis*) as designating both an organ of speech and an organ of hearing and balance; thus as tied up, inseparably, with a fantasy of both mute mouth and deaf ear. My study of this phonocentric[8] fantasy is confined to modern and so-called postmodern Western philosophy, and to its discourse on the university, which I approach by way of the work of Derrida. My study begins in chapter 2 from a point where the threshold between medieval and modern has finally been crossed. Significantly, it was discovery of the ear *os* by Andreas Vesalius that, as much as the Cartesian eye/I, took Western culture over this threshold. The moment of discovery was not without trauma: Vesalius, while cleaning a skeleton— in preparation, no doubt, for the *Fabrica*, his revolutionary treatise on the human body (*De Humani Corporis Fabrica*), published in 1543, the same year that Copernicus's new cosmology (*De Revolutionibus Orbium Coelestium*) also introduced the modern world—was startled when an ossicle fell out of its skull. And here too, the trauma leads to a narrative of loss: in the second skull, the one Vesalius turned next to examine, he could not find the stirrup.[9] Missing an ossicle, that ear must have been deaf; whether it was the ear of a woman is not known.[10] We do know, however, that it was Gabriello Fallopio, the first anatomist to fully open the tympanum and peer into the labyrinth, who discovered and sur-named the female "fallopian tubes." Not just on the threshold of modernity, but "everywhere and at all times," Derrida writes in "Tympan," sexual investments "powerfully constrain the *discourse of the ear*" (MP xiv).

In the text I read in chapter 2, Immanuel Kant stoops and, almost losing his balance, picks up (on) the stirrup. The incident is recorded in a footnote to *The Conflict of the Faculties* (1798) which, with the exception of the *Anthropology*, was Kant's last book, written in his old age and, as he says in the footnote, at a time when he was experiencing weakening on his left side, blurring in his left eye, and difficulty with his organs of balance. Significantly, the note on the stirrup has to do with the question of how to keep a body balanced, how to secure its footing, left and right, particularly at the moment when it has a wide threshold to cross. In *The Conflict of the Faculties*, Kant develops an architecture for the research university, a design that he says will provide the institution with new and secure footings, and with the leverage it needs to cross the threshold from medieval to modern. Adopted at the turn of the century by the University of Berlin, and then transported to North America, Kant's design became foundational for the modern research university as we know it. In keeping with the ocularcentric moment in which it was conceived, Kant's is a design for a panopticon, a vertical institution that puts philosophy at the center and top and that gives it a view of all the academic fields. As I read *The Conflict*, however, Kant is concerned even more with the university's ear than its eye. My reading is guided by Derrida's "*Mochlos*" (a word that designates something monstrous, an animal-human hybrid, a being that lacks the *animus*).

In *The Conflict*, it is the fear of losing his voice that, as a kind of Medusa-effect, leaves Kant and the Kantian university with a speechless mouth. For at each stage of his university design—a labyrinth architecture that gives the institution the shape of an inner ear— Kant withdraws himself further into the interior of the place, constructing a hierarchy of the disciplines by way of charting this inward movement. By the time he arrives at the university's center, which is also its uppermost site, Kant imagines himself—or at least his essential self, his voice-consciousness, which is also supposed to be the university's essence or *animus*—to be withdrawn from exteriority altogether. At this very centerpoint, the point on which all the weight of the structure rests, and the source from which the life of the body comes, Kant's fully withdrawn voice thus falls silent, and the university, for which he, as rational philosopher, is the sole spokesperson, is, in effect, struck dumb.

"The moment of crisis is always the moment of signs," is the way that Derrida puts it in *Speech and Phenomena* (81). Better still, the moment of crisis is the moment of the signifier, the moment when Kant's voice would be released, embodied in a word or gesture, and let go out into the world. But rather than lose his voice, rather than "risk death [of the *animus*] in the body of a signifier that is given over to the world and the visibility of space" (SP 77–78), Kant collapses the distance between his mind and his speech and so stops any movement of sound through his body. It's as if his tongue had been cut off. Lynn Enterline, in her study of the *Metaphorphoses*, notes that Ovid repeatedly evokes the idea of a speechless mouth in order to suggest that the link between mind and voice is at best fragile and easily broken; that voice and lips "are less than, or perhaps more than, mere instruments of the mind" (Enterline 2000, 46). Perhaps it is a sense of this fragility, and a refusal of it, that leads Kant to define himself and the essence of the university over-against an outside Babel of sounds and signs. Or, perhaps Kant's phonocentric fantasy is an instance of what Freud called the "work of mourning," where the subject, out of longing for the lost object, chooses to phantasmically ingest or incorporate it (Freud 1984; see also Abraham and Torok 1987). In this case, mourning would be a work of swallowing the voice and of making it an uncanny presence that haunts the university crypt.

Kant's university is petrified as a result of oral trauma; but the institution's death really comes through the ear. For it is hearing that he first of all disembodies and makes even more ideal than speech, leaving the university deaf even before it becomes mute. In the phonocentric institution, hearing, fully idealized as *hearing-oneself-speak*, has priority: to be a full and free rational subject is "to hear" in advance of speech, writing, or gesture. "*The voice is heard*" by a subject who does not first "have to pass forth beyond himself," as Derrida notes in *Speech and Phenomena* (76). Phonic signs, or "acoustical images," as Saussure would later call them, "are heard [*entendus* = 'heard' plus 'understood'] by the subject who proffers them in the absolute proximity of their present" (76). This acoustic proximity is supposed to be what animates Kant's voice, and the Kantian institution, from within: "My words are 'alive' because they seem not to leave me: not to fall outside me, outside my breath, at a visible distance; not to cease to belong to me, to be at my disposition 'without further props'" (76). And it is this acoustic proximity—and loss of proximity—that determines the placement of the disciplines in Kant's university hierarchy. Pure rational philosophy, with its claim to hear the voice of reason in a wholly nonexterior way, is granted full supervisory title at the university's center and top; while the faculties of law, medicine, and theology, rooted as they are in empirical experience, their ears tuned to the outside world, are assigned a lower place; some distance removed from the center, they are university's necessary supplements or props.

It is important to remember that Kant's retreat into the proximity of *hearing-oneself-speak* is actually a blueprint for the subordination of space and the movement of spacing, so that the privileged interior, from which speech, writing, and gesture are excluded, is not a space at all, but an absence of space, "a self-proximity that would in fact be the absolute reduction of space" (SP 79). Philosophy's look-out at the top of the edifice is, then, what Derrida refers to as a "non-place" (LIP 132; see also Wigley 1993, 69), where the subject, and so the institution, is finally and fully estranged from the sound of its own voice and from the spacing movement that this sound is. Since, without movement, no embodied hearing can take place, the university ends up with both its tongue and ear cut off. Kant, who always puts philosophy on the left, leaves us with an institution that is weakened on this side, and that, with its inner ear disabled, suffers from problems of balance. We could even say, given this erosion of the interior, that the modern university is born not only still, *still-born*, but also stooped over. At its inauguration, the institution is already in danger of falling.

Kant's subordination (incorporation) of space and spacing is, as a Medusa-effect, his defense against loss of an imagined oral-aural proximity: "The proximity is broken when, instead of hearing myself speak, I see myself write or gesture" (SP 80). Out of the same anxiety about lost proximity, he insists on a strict separation of philosophy from the other university faculties, and even on a division within philosophy itself, a boundary that would separate pure reason from branches of the discipline (historical philosophy, for instance) that clothe reason in empirical knowledge. The same phonocentric fantasy of proximity prompts Kant to establish a rigorous, uncrossable, *us/them* boundary between the university and the outside world. With this boundary, he is determined to exclude from the university a disparate group, some of whom are beholden not so much to reason as to political and utilitarian concerns; some of whom are either too distracted or too incompetent—idiots (*Idioten*), Kant calls them—to listen to the voice of reason. Even more than those who do not listen, however, this inside/outside boundary banishes those who cannot hear. Deafness is a more serious loss than blindness, Kant explains in the *Anthropology*, published in the same year as *The Conflict*. For even if a man loses his hearing later in life, and is able to compensate for the loss by use of his eyes, "whether to observe mimicry or, even more mediately to read a text" (Kant 1974, 38), or by using his sense of sight together with touch—"He can also use his eyes to read our lips, or his sense of touch to feel our lip movements in the dark" (37)— loss of hearing leaves one, from then on, outside of self-presence, dependent on embodied signifiers and empirical prostheses. More drastically still, the man deaf from birth, who has not yet heard the voice of reason speak within him, who has never *heard-himself-speak*, cannot arrive at an idea. There is no place for the so-called deaf and dumb inside the academic institution, for "a man who, because he was deaf from birth, must also remain dumb (without speech) can never achieve more than an *analogue* of reason" (34).

It is not incidental, then, that, as Lennard Davis contends, "Europe became deaf" in the eighteenth century (Davis 1995, 51), at the very moment when the modern research university was born. Despite the received opinion of historians, philosophers, and critics that deafness is an "epiphenomenon," all but irrelevant to the study of Enlightenment thought and culture, it developed in the eighteenth century into a matter of central interest, Davis points out. Michel Foucault in *Madness and Civilization* shows how, at the close of the Middle Ages, the targeting and confinement of "madness" provided a discourse out of which the new "rationality" could emerge. In much the same way, Davis suggests, during the eighteenth century "deafness" was constituted as a fascinating otherness—an "icon," as he calls it—against which Enlightenment ideas about "subject, class position, and the body" could be confirmed (Davis 51). The disabled *os*, the deaf ear, and therefore the mute mouth, is this kind of icon for Kant in *The Conflict*: a figure of loss against which he withdraws, and defines, the rational subject and the institution of reason. What I must add to Davis's point is this: the icon sets up a Medusa-effect, in that Kant's withdrawal into a disembodied oral and aural ideal leaves the modern university unable to speak or hear.

THE SCHOLARLY SIGNATURE

Despite the argument that vision has sole hegemony in the modern era (Jay 1994, 14), Kant's *The Conflict of the Faculties* designs the research university as the product of a phonocentric imaginary, thus as much an audiocentric, as an ocularcentric, institution. A generation after Kant, the work of that other great philosopher-architect of modernity, Georg Wilhelm Friedrich Hegel, also casts doubt on the thesis that, in the shift from medieval to modern, the voice and ear are left behind. With his grand narrative of history as the coming to light out of darkness and the return journey of spirit (*Geist*), rising first in the East, then setting in the intelligible eye of the Westerner, the prominence of light and sight in Hegel cannot be questioned. In Hegel, we have what Derrida calls philosophy-as-photology, "a history of, or treatise on, light" (WD 27). We have, then, the same affiliation between the metaphor of the sun and the metaphors of circle and seed that Derrida says permeates all of Western metaphysics. The eye is generally taken to be at the center of this tropological system: the solar, patriarchal eye/I and its light as what William Spanos calls the "foundational trope" out of which "radiate" the allotropes of the centered circle and the seed (which includes both planting/cultivation and phallic insemination) (Spanos 2000, 14). To this systemic metaphorics, however, I would add sound and hearing, not just as additional allotropes of light/sight, but the eye, rather, as allotrope of the ear. For spirit's determination as light, separated from the empirical world, is too abstract, too "Kantian," for Hegel; rather than withdrawing the essence of being from the substantial world, Hegel has ideality pass through material bodies—portraying the great story of spirit's journey of return-to-itself as a story of the idealizing-relief of sound. Spirit is the sound-source: and from the moment that its light (seed) first enters the Eastern darkness and immerses itself in matter, it is spirit's *oscillation-vibration* that puts history on its course. Granted, the heavy matter of the East barely stirs when entered by spirit, but as its spiral passages take it from East to West, as it returns ever closer to its self, the progress of spirit is charted, by Hegel, as the passage of sound—from silence through noise and voice to "active" (inseminating) speech; speech that, in a final passage, is relieved into *savoir absolu* (this is Derrida's translation in *Glas* of "absolute spirit," his siglum for which is *Sa*. I must add that *Sa* is, as a Medusa-effect, *silence absolute*).

Hegel's philosophy "demonstrates very clearly the strange privilege of sound in idealization, the production of the concept and the self-presence of the subject," Derrida writes in *Of Grammatology*, following his remark with a quotation from Hegel's *Aesthetics*: "'This ideal motion, in which through the sound what is as it were the simple subjectivity [*Subjektivität*], the soul of the material thing expresses itself, the ear receives also in a theoretical [*theoretisch*] way, just as the eye shape and colour, thus allowing the interiority of the object to become interiority itself [*läßt dadurch das Innere der Gegenstände für das Innere selbst werden*]'" (OG 12). Given that sound is this spirit or "soul of the material thing," hearing, the sense through which the mechanical and material becomes ideal, is more privileged than sight, as Hegel himself states in his *Aesthetics* (II, 890). I think Hegel's privileging of hearing lies behind his morbid fascination with the Egyptian Sphinx, the massive stone animal-human hybrid that, in common with the Medusa, shows us a female face that is stone deaf, and therefore dumb. Although they are turned toward the sun, as if waiting for spirit to give them sound, these colossal stone statues remain "motionless" and "mute" (I, 354), their brute ears too heavy to enable spirit's oscillation to resound as intelligible speech. This speech would be phonetic—not the mysterious sign language of Egyptian hieroglyphics, the language that Hegel finds as enigmatic as the expression the Sphinx wears on her face. Kant, in his *Anthropology*, bars the deaf and dumb from the rational sphere because they lack the "words" in which the voice of reason is first heard and then spoken (Kant 1974, 34). Even more than Kant, Hegel privileges phonetic speech, preeminently his own German tongue, the national work of his own world-historical people, as the mode in which an inmost self first resonates, and then resounds, with spirit's presence. In Egypt, "[a] national work in the department of language is wanting" (Hegel 1991a, 199). While its hieroglyph symbols can be partially phonetic, and so bring it closer than China to the *us* of the *us/them* boundary that separates Occident from Orient, what is inside from what is outside of world-history, Egypt remains, at best, a transitional phase, a mediating moment. Its hybrid hieroglyphs hint at spirit's struggle to free itself from nature, but in the end, they are as speechless as the silent face of the Sphinx, "mysterious and dumb, mute and motionless, because here spirit itself has not really found its own inner life and cannot speak the clear and distinct language of spirit" (Hegel 1975 I, 354).

The fate of Hegel's woman is given in the Egyptian Sphinx, a matter that concerns me in chapter 3, where, by way of reading Derrida's *Glas*, I approach Hegel's university—approach but do not enter, for as a woman who lacks an active voice-hearing apparatus, I am (doubly) banned from the place. According to Hegel, a woman belongs to the home and the hearth because, like the Sphinx, incapable of vibrating freely with herself, she is impotent: she has a speechless mouth. Also like the Sphinx, which crosses female breasts and face with animal paws and wings, she is a hybrid creature, part above ground, part below: in the family, the woman's transitional role is to facilitate the passage, through her body, of seed (speech) from father to son, in which capacity, she mediates, albeit passively, the idealizing progress of spirit (the passage from voice to *hearing-oneself-speak*); but as the son passes on beyond the family to higher education, the woman (mother, daughter) falls back to the underground, her law being dumb-darkness: she has to take her light from the man. Heavy matter to his free spiritual self, the woman is keeper of the man's tomb, the one who shrouds and buries his corpse, attends to his memorialization, and ends up herself, quite simply, dead. Incapable of passing into universality, the woman, in Hegel's family, is a disappearing middle term.

In chapter 3, I focus on Hegel's family, as Derrida does in *Glas*, in the first instance because, where there is, as Hegel has it, no family in Kant, one cannot get to university in Hegel without a passage through the family—the family as a determinate moment, what in his *Philosophy of Right*, he describes as the first and most "natural" moment of *Sittlichkeit*. We find the university here: education is the family's third and final stage, the stage through which, having produced and passed on its sons, the family-as-moment comes to an end. But even though the family-as-family ceases to be—in the passage to education of sons—the family-as-structure goes on: and this is the main reason why, following Derrida in *Glas*, I focus on the family in chapter 3.

Indeed, even as the son passes beyond the family, so as to accomplish the relief of the father and bring the family circle to a close, the familial structure is immediately repeated in the classroom, where education takes the form of rearing (raising the father's spirit in) the son. "The father [spirit, self, subject] divides, goes out of himself into his son, recognizes himself in the son, and finds himself again, re-counts himself in his revenue" (G 28ai). The family provides the model for Hegel's pedagogy. More than that, the family gets repeated in—is the "copulative" structure of—every *Aufhebung*. "The whole system repeats itself in the family" (G 20a). Spirit's return journey through history, Hegel's overarching narrative of sound, is itself an absolute Christian Holy Family scene: the going-forth-from-himself of the father, coming-back-to-himself in the son, a conception that passes through, even as it incorporates/crosses out, the woman, the material-middle term. Every return-to-self passage of sound-become-speech (spirit, seed) through a signifier is an instance of this familial relief; each time, the embodied middle is consumed.

In approaching Hegel's university through Derrida's reading of this familial structure in *Glas*, my main interest is in the woman, the middle that disappears. Because she is a speechless *os*, because she lacks the "voice of active hearing" (G 250a), Hegel's woman is a Medusa-figure against which he defines male subjectivity and male pedagogy. At the same time, as was the case with Kant, this fantasy of aural/oral lack sets up a Medusa-effect: for in consuming the em-bodied middle of which woman is the trope, Hegel stops the male subject's outer ear and cuts off his voice. This is what happens in the passage to *Sa*, the Absolute Idea that Hegel's signature is, where all exteriority disappears into silence absolute. As with Kant, so with Hegel, then, where the essence of being is proximity-to-self, where being is "being-(close)-by-itself" (G 23a), hearing is privileged as *hearing-oneself-speak*, with the effect—the Medusa effect—that voice and ear are disembodied.

As will be evident by now, I am interested throughout this book in the "re-embodiment" of hearing, this as inseparable from the task of university re-founding. For although hearing has, of course, never left the body, the idealizing narratives of modernity tell another story, one that structures and supports oppressive academic and political institutions—themselves part of "discourse," always discursively made and sustained. To argue for embodied hearing—whether by oralism or gesturalism, by lip reading or hand signing—is to situate "being" in relation to an other-outside. Audibility, I will argue, requires exteriority: *no hearing without an outside*. It involves vibrations—their differentiating-spacing movement—that transmit through a medium (despite the contention of Donald Lowe, hearing is never unmediated, not any more so in an "oral-aural" than in an "ocular" culture) and that imprint on a body, a tympanum, or other writing pad: *no hearing without an imprint of some sort*. I will also argue, as does Derrida with his notion of *proto-writing* ("there is no linguistic sign before writing" [OG 14]), that the imprint is there from the start; it does not invade or detract from an original, *hearing-oneself-speak*, interiority; and it does not disappear, at the "end" (as the circle returns to itself) into an idealized voice-consciousness. The imprint *remains*, as does Derrida's unmistakably graphic, better still, hieroglyphic, countersignature in *Glas*: an imprint that is at once *seen* zigzagging and *heard* tolling back and forth between the book's left and right columns. This signature's bastard course is a coming-going movement that thwarts education's return-to-self father-son familial relief, and that—even as they are being put in place—shakes the university's foundations.

INSTITUTIONS OF THE "YES"

Derrida suggests that all of Heidegger's work can be read "as a drama of sorting things out with the university" (CM 209). In this book, the drama makes for something of a hinge. For as I discuss in chapter 4, there is, in Heidegger's work, a gesture of silencing-deletion that drives the modern concept of university to the edge of an abyss and that takes the Medusa-effect I have been tracking in this university discourse to a terrifying extreme. Yet there is also in Heidegger a silence that has to do with writing differentially, "under erasure" or within what Derrida calls "mute signs." This kind of silencing suggests opening and response-ability to an other-outside; thus, it is a pivot on which the university might turn, as it were, from a phonocentric fantasy of loss to a discourse that re-embodies hearing. In chapter 4, my reading of Derrida's hearing of Heidegger on the university is situated between these two gestures of silence. Given the argument I am proposing in this book—that there can be no hearing without movement and an imprint of some sort—I think it important to note that each of the two types of silence entails imprinting, a "typological motif" (OS 34), although only one allows the imprint to space-oscillate.

Chapter 4 locates the first gesture of silencing in Heidegger's 1933 Rectorate Address, delivered on the occasion of his installation as Rector of the University of Freiburg. While the Rectorate Address "confirms something essential" to the Kantian concept of the university, Derrida suggests, it also represents that concept's "limit" (CM 209), I would say, end.[11] In a discourse that gathers ideal being close to himself, and to an identifiable "us," and that sanctions Nazism in the same gesture, Heidegger's Address exalts spirit (*Geist*)—as what affirms itself through the spiritual world (*geistige Welt*) of the German people, through the will-to essence of the German university, and through the self-affirming speech of its new *spiritus rector* (see OS, chapter V; Heidegger 1985).[12] Just as Hegel praised the national and spiritual institution of the German language, in the Rectorate Address, "[t]he German character of this university is not a secondary or contingent predicate," Derrida maintains; "it cannot be dissociated from this affirmation of spirit. As the highest agency of the institution thus erected, of this 'high school' (*hohe Schule*), directed upwards from the heights, spirit can do nothing other than affirm itself—and this, as we shall hear, in the movement of an authentication or identification which *wish themselves to be properly* German" (OS 33). The identification-authentication is rendered with the all-out force of a "single blow" (31) that withdraws the Rector's speech (and, therefore, hearing) into a spiritual beyond, and so *deafens* Heidegger, even as—in this limit-case of the Medusa effect—he is *dumbstruck*. Once the blow, the "spiritual imprint" (38), is delivered, once, in a simultaneous celebration of spirit, sanctioning of Nazism, and reestablishing of metaphysics, the limit is met, Heidegger falls forever silent: deaf from then on to the question of his, and the university's, responsibility vis-à-vis Nazism, mute on the question unto his death.

In the Rectorate Address, the speechless *os* from which Heidegger withdraws, and to which he opposes a spiritualized Nazism and the spiritual essence of the German university, belongs, I argue in chapter 4, not immediately to a woman, but to the benumbed animal with which she has been historically conflated, as in Hegel, for instance. The othering of "the animal" is already underway in Heidegger's lecture course of 1929–30, *The Fundamental Concepts of Metaphysics*, which, in this respect, is "preparatory" to the Rectorate Address. What

Heidegger wants to talk about in the lecture course—the fundamental way of life, the *life as-such*, of *Dasein*—can be got at, he says, only by way of distinguishing between the world-poor animal and man, between "what constitutes the *essence of the animality* of the animal and the *essence of the humanity* of man" (Heidegger 1995, 179). This (*us/ them*) distinction can be delimited, he says, by philosophy only, not by the other university disciplines, certainly not by the psychological, biological, and physical sciences; what he means by "life," for instance, "*'life' as such cannot in principle be grasped from within the perspectives of these disciplines*" (188). In broaching the question of the as-such, then, Heidegger immediately, and with one and the same sweeping gesture, reconstitutes the Kantian hierarchy of the university disciplines and reinstates the binary man/animal opposition. The stone, since it has "no being at all" (179), is not really the other pole of Heidegger's binary opposition; it is the animal, rather, on which his phonocentric fantasy fixes, the animal that, after all, does have life and does relate to the world around it, but—because it does not have speech and hearing, because "benumbedness" (*Benommenheit*), the *essence* of the animal state, is "deaf and dumb"—in a way that Heidegger wants to distinguish absolutely from the "being-there" of *Dasein*. The gesture of removing the benumbed animal to the absolute outside of the as-such is repeated, emphatically, in 1935, at the opening of *An Introduction to Metaphysics*, where, as Derrida points out in *Of Spirit*, Heidegger declares both that "[t]he world is always a *spiritual* world," and, in the very next sentence, that "the animal has no world." It follows, Derrida says, that "the animal has no spirit, since, as we have just read, every world is spiritual. Animality is not *of spirit*" (OS 47). The spirit that the benumbed animal does not have is the spirit that the Rectorate Address celebrates. The celebration "corresponds properly, literally, to an *exaltation* of the spiritual," Derrida writes. "It is an elevation" (39) of everything Heidegger consecrates as "spiritual" to the highest remove from everything that he associates with "the animal."

In keeping with the operation of what I have been calling the Medusa effect, Heidegger's spiritualizing of being in the Rectorate Address, a move that deafens him and leaves him forever silent, is, on its other side, the abjection and reification of a disabled *os*—an *os* that is labeled as "animal," but that, through the oppositional binary that it inscribes, belongs as much to the woman, perhaps also to the man of science who, like the animal, is lacking "the hand." By the same token, the "spiritual imprint" with which, in a single stroke, Heidegger sanctions Nazism and exalts the highest forces of the German university, the spiritual guides of *die hohe Schule*, is, on its other side, a forceful mark of deletion (*Durchstreichung*) that strikes the animal out—and for the reason that the animal lacks "our" tongue. Heidegger's fantasy of withdrawal into spirit and the realm of the "as-such" recalls the words of Mieke Bal with which I opened this chapter: that in the Medusa story, the other, animal-body-woman, is reified and ends up dead.

That said, Derrida (in *Of Spirit* and in the *Geschlecht* papers he has published thus far) goes on to locate a second gesture of silencing in Heidegger, a gesture that, while it involves an imprinting, is utterly different from Heidegger's animal crossing-out. For one thing, this second gesture does not affirm spirit, but rather "avoids" its invocation. This is the gesture that, Derrida says, is made by the Heidegger of *Being and Time*, the Heidegger who would distinguish his analytic of *Dasein* from all *pneumatology*. For this Heidegger, "In order to say what we are, who we are, it appears to be indispensable to *avoid* all the concepts in the subjective or *subjectal* series: in particular that of spirit" (OS 17). The latter word, if used at all in Heidegger's analytic, must be, as it were, crossed through, written "silently" (25) within nonphonetic, non-acoustic quotation marks; Derrida calls them "mute signs" (25). My discussion in chapter 4 of this "silencing" of spirit, and the relation it has to Heidegger's mutism in *Being and Time* on the question of sexual difference, picks up on Derrida's reading in "*Geschlecht*: sexual difference, ontological difference" of Heidegger's 1928 lecture course on logic. In the course, then again in *Being and Time* and in later texts, Derrida locates an imprinting that is "radically different" (54) from the Heideggerian *Durchstreichung*. This stroke is double and nondual and, in keeping with my thesis that embodied hearing requires an "originary" imprinting, it marks *Dasein* from the start, suggesting that life begins already "written," rather than from the Kantian-Hegelian proximity of *hearing-oneself-speak*. That it would be impossible, starting from this "originary de-propriation" (80), to set up phonocentrism's acoustic-phonetic fantasy, is a point that Derrida explores further in his fourth *Geschlecht*, "Heidegger's Ear: Philopolemology (*Geschlecht* IV)," and with particular reference to a parenthetical passage in *Being and Time* on "hearing the voice of the friend," a voice that, Derrida suggests, cannot be "reduced to the phoneme or to the acoustic phenomenon" (GIV 174). To hear the voice of Heidegger's friend is to allow for, and affirm, its "there-and-back, the going-and-coming" (183) *movement*, the spacing of its call (*Ruf*). I am taken with Derrida's claim that listening and responding—"yes"—to this voice that "goes and comes; here, toward presence, there, toward absence" (167) makes of *being-there* a matter of being carried, *bei-sich*, beside, alongside, or outside of oneself, "beyond the acoustic phenomenon" to "what is outside us" (178).

INTERLACE

With Derrida's reading of the *bei-sich* as "being outside" of an anthropomorphic, linguistic, or national "us," the concept of academic freedom, and responsibility, always central to the analysis I undertake in this book, assumes some "animal," or to use Derrida's word, some "anhuman," quality (CM 205). In chapter 5, responsibility has to do with things that are "inanimate"—shoes—and with the debated question of how such mute things, once painted, gain speech. The debate in question also concerns the demarcation of terms—"modern" and "postmodern" as chief among these—and issues of ownership and restitution—chiefly of shoes painted by Vincent van Gogh and discussed by Heidegger in *The Origin of the Work of Art*. I read this as a debate about university foundations, and not just because it takes place between university professors.

I enter the debate by way of Fredric Jameson's contention in *Postmodernism, or, the Cultural Logic of Late Capitalism* that "van Gogh's well-known painting of the peasant shoes" (Jameson 1991, 6) is a canonical work of high modernist art that, through inert things, peasant shoes, enacts a transformative, utopian gesture. Since, Jameson says, this is precisely Heidegger's interpretation of "the painting" (which painting Jameson has under discussion I consider to be anything but clear) in *The Origin of the Work of Art*, what he calls "the van Gogh-Heidegger shoes" (10) form a matching pair—and this, I suggest, is because they provide shoes that fit Jameson perfectly well. In an act of critical ventriloquism, Jameson attributes his own voice to "the van Gogh-Heidegger shoes," claiming that the shoes *speak* the truth of his historical-materialist, high-modernist "deep" reading of art. Introducing a fourth to this Heidegger-van Gogh-Jameson scene does not give us another pair: for when Jameson contemplates the shoes of Andy Warhol, he does not see his match. On the contrary, Warhol's *Dia-*

mond Dust Shoes are "mute," Jameson claims: detached from a subject, uncoupled, fetishes, they are "postmodern"—dead objects—into which Jameson cannot drop his voice. (The founding moment, we must remember, is always a moment of sexual difference.)

From Jameson's analysis of the "truth in painting," I turn to one that Derrida takes up in "Restitutions," one involving a scene that, as he puts it, "both is and is not very academic, between two Jewish professors who fled the Nazis; and it involves Heidegger as well, his peasant ideology, the question of the subject and a crowd of ghosts, some of whom came back from the death camps in their shoes" (CM 207). It is just where his peasant ideology surfaces in *The Origin* that, according to Meyer Schapiro, one of the Jewish professors, Heidegger misses the truth in the van Gogh painting, and does so by misappropriating the painted shoes. The shoes don't belong to a peasant, says Schapiro (who was alerted to *The Origin* by the other Jewish professor, Kurt Goldstein, his friend; and who now disputes the ownership in writing to Heidegger); contrary to Heidegger's interpretation, the shoes are the artist's own. Considering this difference of opinion between Heidegger and Schapiro as to who owns the painted shoes, entering as a fourth party to the debate I set up in chapter 5, Derrida does not line up on either side so as to give us a pair. Rather, as I suggest in this chapter, it is pairing itself with which Derrida takes issue, the correspondence that both Heidegger and Schapiro display in their difference over who owns the shoes. Each party to the debate—Heidegger, in those passages of *The Origin* that dwell, in pathos, on "a pair of peasant shoes," Schapiro, in attributing the shoes to the signatory of the work—sees the van Gogh shoes as a self-portrait (a bandaged self-portrait, Derrida ventures). As does Jameson, each party to the Schapiro-Heidegger pair ventriloquizes the shoes, has them hear, and then speak, restitute, the interpreter's owned truth.

For Derrida, Heidegger's *The Origin of the Work of Art*, despite its pathos and its naïveté in identifying the owner of the shoes, is not simply an instrument of "modernity," as Jameson takes it to be. Nor, for Derrida, is *The Origin* "postmodern," at least not in Jameson's sense of an historical-capitalist sequel. However, if we define the term, not epochally, but as a *mode of response* where, as Jean-François Lyotard puts it, "writing [painting, speaking, gesturing] is the testimony of a fracture, of the opening onto the other" (Lyotard 1988, 113), then *The Origin*, for Derrida, could be read as a "hinge" text on which the university, and its professors, might turn from a "modern" to a "postmodern" discursivity. Because he is interested in "opening unto the other," Derrida, in "Restitutions," does not attempt to resolve the issue of the ownership of the shoes. He dwells, rather, on laces. These laces are important to my discussion in chapter 5: both the ones that are painted to exceed, or fall outside of, the frame and so to figure the crossing of what would separate an inside from an out, an *us* from a *them*; and the ones whose interlacing movement leaves its mark of passage in *The Origin of the Work of Art*, thereby introducing a dissymmetry to the Schapiro-Heidegger pair. In the lacing, Derrida suggests, a *trait* is painted/inscribed. And it is in the embodied experience of the *trait*—as spacing—that Derrida locates, in *The Origin*, a political and critical resistance to authorial truth. Similarly, in "Restitutions," it is spacing that upsets the phonocentric fantasy of a voice that begins with, and returns to, a first-person self. Some of this spacing is visible, for "Restitutions," a text without obvious beginning or end, is, as Derrida says, a "polylogue (for n + 1—female—voices)" (TP 256), voices that spatialize themselves on the page. At the same time, a dimension of the text's spacing is not so much seen ("I am not sure that space is essentially mastered by [*livré à*] the look" [SA 24]) as it is felt— I would say, *heard*—in the oscillating movement, the imprinting of the *trait*. Where "[t]he voice separates," Derrida says, we are no longer subsuming hearing to linguistic-phonetic privilege or presence to self; "it is a differential vibration that at the same time interrupts, hinders, prevents access, maintains a distance" (23). We are, here, crossing the limits of the phonocentric institution, folding its outside in.

AN OTHER EAR

Moving from the mutism of the animal in chapter 4, through the matter, in chapter 5, of animating shoes with speech, I turn (back) in chapter 6 to the presumed monumental silence of stone—and to architecture. For all the heavy physicality of its constructions, architecture, for Hegel, certainly that cast in stone, *can't speak*; it is not amenable to spirit's oscillations, and not until it becomes habitation does it serve human freedom at all. This Hegelian gesture of putting architecture "in service"—in the service of metaphysics and thus of the ideal of proximity that I maintain both disembodies hearing and stigmatizes deafness—is a gesture that Heidegger repeats, and that

Derrida opposes. "My objection to Heidegger," Derrida says, "often begins with the spatial arts. That is because I think that the hierarchization of the arts he practices in his discourse on art and painting, or on poetry, repeats a classical philosophical gesture, and that is exactly what I argue against" (SA 25). Since, as I have been arguing, the hierarchization of the arts also operates in the modern discourse on the university—where architecture, along with the physical sciences, is weighed down at the bottom, and poetry-conducting-to-philosophy has proximity at the top—no "deconstruction" of modernity's discourse of institution can avoid the tradition's subordination of architecture to (phonetic) poetic speech. I take this issue up in chapter 6, where I note, via Paul Ricoeur's *The Rule of Metaphor*, that the role Kant assumes for himself in *The Conflict of the Faculties* as university architect is still very much in vogue in contemporary philosophy. At the same time, as we see in Alberto Pérez-Gómez's "*Chora*, the Space of Architectural Representation," today's architect has also learned to position himself as a new philosopher-poet. In Pérez-Gómez's case, the philosopher returns us to metaphysics, to the same origin and *telos* that Ricoeur advocates in *The Rule of Metaphor*. If I resist the theory of metaphor that is common to Pérez-Gómez and Ricoeur, it is for reason of this phonocentric return. For all the spacing and movement they advocate, both, by way of metaphor, reconstitute a philosophy of self-presence.

The site of the collaboration I discuss in chapter 6 is the Parc de la Villette "campus" in France. Here, on a large 125 acre expanse in the northeast corner of Paris, Bernard Tschumi began work in 1983 on a dissociated or dispersed building, an architectural endeavor that attempts to dissociate or decenter modernity's idea of the authorial and self-present subject. The principle of disjunction extends as well to the signified-signifier relation, for the basic building block at la Villette is an empty red box; Tschumi calls it a *folie*. The *folie* on which I focus in chapter 6 is a "garden" that Derrida and architect Peter Eisenman designed together for la Villette. The garden, *Chora L*, is constructed entirely of stone and in the shape of a lyre, the stringed instrument that the Sirens used to accompany their song to Odysseus—who blocked men's ears so as to mute the Sirens' voices. The shape and lore of the lyre is also based on Plato's *chora*, the imprint-bearer that shakes or vibrates in the *Timaeus*, inscribing a winnowing movement in his text. I am interested in reading the way this movement "inscribes itself in stone" (Pf 70) in the Derrida-Eisenman garden, partly through the *mise-en-abyme* that layers the lyres, one inside another, carrying us back through successive historical myths of the woman's open and malevolent mouth. It's the movement that transforms these stories and that opens the university's ears to hear.

TWO

THE ARCHITECTURE OF INSTITUTION

The university is a (finished) product, I would almost call it the child
of an inseparable couple, metaphysics and technology. At the least, the
university furnished the space or the topological configuration for such
an offspring. It is a paradox that, at the moment when such offspring
overflows the places assigned it, and the university becomes small and
old, its "idea" reigns everywhere, more and better than ever.

—Derrida, "Mochlos; or, The Conflict of the Faculties"

IMMANUEL KANT WAS PONDERING the idea of the university, the
meaning of the terms *university* and *responsibility*, the relation of one
to the other, when over two centuries ago, he wrote *The Conflict of
the Faculties* (*Der Streit der Fakultäten* 1798), a text that opens with the
words, "Whoever it was that first hit on the notion of the university
and proposed that a public institution of this kind be established, it
was not a bad idea . . ." (Kant 1979, 23). *It was not a bad idea*, Kant
says, to fasten on a rule of division, "a division of labor," by which to
order the university faculties, "so that for every branch of the sciences
there would be a public teacher or *professor* appointed as its trustee,
and all of these together would form a kind of learned community
called a *university*" (23). The university would have to have autonomy,
he adds, "since only scholars can pass judgment on scholars as such"
(23), and since only reason, free of public and political influence, can
form the institution as a whole.

Elaborating on the architecture of such a teaching institution
that would be governed by autonomous reason, *The Conflict of the*

27

Faculties spells out what Richard Rand calls "the blueprint for the modern research university" (Rand 1992, vii). In Germany, Kant's blueprint led to Wilhelm von Humboldt's 1810 plan for the University of Berlin, Rand notes, and to writings on the academic institution by Schelling, Fichte, Schopenhauer, Nietzsche, and Heidegger, becoming so successful a model that it was adopted at the end of the century by American universities as well. And yet, despite its success as a university charter, *The Conflict of the Faculties* was either "utterly ignored" (viii) by Kant scholars or else relegated to the margins as a minor essay that "contains no important new ideas" (Greene 1980, lxxii). This indifference to Kant's treatise was challenged by Derrida's "*Mochlos*; or The Conflict of the Faculties," a lecture he delivered at a Columbia University symposium celebrating the centennial of its graduate school. Derrida's lecture provided the impetus for a 1987 conference on *The Conflict of the Faculties* that was held at the University of Alabama, "Our Academic Contract: *The Conflict of the Faculties* in America," the published papers from which, edited by Rand, include an interview with Derrida on the university as well as a translation of his Columbia lecture.[1] In "*Mochlos*," then, Derrida reopens *The Conflict of the Faculties*. He does so for the reason that, to use his words, "the *fatum* of responsibility seems inscribed there at the origin, on the very eve of the modern university, in its pre-inaugural address. It is inscribed there in language receiving from Kant its first great illustration, its first conceptual formulation of major rigor and consequence" (M 10).

In the present chapter, I take Kant's *The Conflict of the Faculties* to be a founding text. It provides the conceptual and architectural design for the modern research university, including a plan for the university disciplines, their placement and relation one to the other; and it delineates the terms under which the university should deal with the outside world. Such founding is just what Kant intended in *The Conflict*: with his blueprint, he proposed to take the university across the threshold from the medieval to the modern age; to give the university body a new and solid footing—and the leverage it needed to make the leap. Not incidentally, *The Conflict* is a work of Kant's old age, written when he was experiencing weakening on his left side, blurring in his left eye, dizziness, and problems with his organs of balance. It's in a discussion of these problems, in a footnote to *The Conflict*, that he fastens on the figure of the lever, the *hypomochlium*, and on leverage, as what the university needs to vault into the modern world. Although it appears only in a marginal note, I will, in this chapter, take the lever to be central to what *The Conflict* is about: my argument is that although Kant wants to design an upright and stable university, secure on its two, left and right, feet, his institution, like the elderly philosopher himself, suffers from dizziness and problems of balance—and this, for the reason that its inner ear is disabled. At every stage of his university design, Kant withdraws himself farther from the outside world, bounding off the university's essence from those who are deaf to reason's voice, and constructing a hierarchy of the disciplines by way of charting this inward movement. This withdrawal could be called a Medusa effect, for it petrifies the university and cuts off its hearing and speech. At the institution's innermost place, which is also its highest reach, the pinnacle from which philosophy exercises visual surveillance over all the university disciplines and over matters of truth in the outside world, the voice of reason makes itself known, speaks and is immediately heard, without any need of physical mouth or embodied ear—and without recourse to signifying materiality. Thus, while Kant's university, as the product of a phonocentric imaginary, is designed in "the form of an ear" and has the structure of a series of "labyrinth, semicircular canals" (MP xviin), just where the institution reaches its animating center and rises to its full height, it finds itself "deaf and dumb."

It is this, modernity's phonocentric concept of university, that Derrida opens to question (and to body) when, in "Mochlos," he reopens *The Conflict of the Faculties*. The issue is not, he says, whether the university needs to be refounded. "We live in a world where the foundation of a new law—in particular a new university law—is necessary" (M 30). Greek for "lever," the title word, *mochlos*, suggests, however, that we can reconstitute the university today only "by seeking leverage, by seeking to use the traditional institution—the extant university—as the point from and by means of which one could spring to a new foundation" (Bahti 1992, 61). *Mochlos* is a work on the lever: "How do we orient ourselves toward the foundation of a new law?" Since it cannot simply break with tradition, how might a new university foundation "negotiate a compromise with the traditional law?" (M 30). Just as Kant in *The Conflict* used the institution he inherited as the lever with which to push off to another university grounding, so Derrida in "Mochlos" takes Kant's text to be the current university's "foundational soil, a support for leaping to another place for founding" (31).[2] Refounding is not a matter of transcending the university from above, but rather of finding new ways to inhabit the institution and the discourse on which it is built. "*Mochlos*" is about such inhabiting from within in the mode of a parasite that "gnaws away at the borders" (MP xxiii) of the Kantian university's partition walls. The *os*, the "*Mochlos*" *os*, that does this "gnawing," turns the conventional Medusan *os mutum* into a mouth that moves; by moving, this mouth makes openings that let the voice inside go out. Although with Kant we are only at the modern university's inauguration, what results from Derrida's "*Mochlos*," as I read it, is an institution already changed. No longer constituted on the fantasy of an erect male body that can stay alive only by *hearing-itself-speak*, the "*Mochlos*" university, as the title word suggests, is a slightly "monstrous" institution: it does not close off the body (animal, woman) and it allows for movement, back and forth, across its frame.[3]

FIRST TURNING: FIGURING THE FRAME

Attention to the boundary that separates the university off from the external world is made necessary, for Kant, by the immediate context of *The Conflict of the Faculties*. Kant wrote the treatise on the occasion of his censorship by the king of Prussia, Friedrich Wilhelm II, for having misused his philosophy to distort certain Christian teachings in *Religion Within the Limits of Reason Alone*. According to king Friedrich's admonishing letter (sent to Kant in October 1794, and cited in his Preface to *The Conflict of the Faculties*), Kant acted "irresponsibly" and against his "duty as a teacher of youth," also violated the "paternal purpose" of his father, the king, by publishing in *Religion Within the Limits of Reason Alone* his criticisms of some of the most fundamental doctrines of Christianity and Holy Scriptures. "We expected better things of you," the king scolds Kant in his letter:

> as you yourself must realize how irresponsibly you have acted against your duty as a teacher of youth and against our paternal purpose, which you know very well. We demand that you give at once a most conscientious account of yourself, and expect that in the future, to avoid our highest disfavor, you will be guilty of no such fault, but rather, in keeping with your duty, apply your

authority and your talents to the progressive realization of our paternal purpose. Failing this, you must expect unpleasant measures for your continuing obstinacy. (Kant 1979, 11)

Even before entering the university, pausing, as it were, on its threshold in his Preface to *The Conflict of the Faculties*, Kant responds to King Friedrich Wilhelm's censoring letter by delimiting *outside* from *in*: Kant does not deny the king his royal right to censor, but he does confine this right of the government to the university's outside. On the outside, in the civic realm, Kant says, the government, charged with securing the harmony and peace of the society under its rule, has the right to sanction religious teachings that are conducive to this end. And since certain tenets of the Bible and Christianity are particularly useful as such means of public instruction, the crown is entitled to sanction these and to ensure that they are appropriately expounded, to censor officers of the church in preaching to their congregations, "those who are appointed to teach the people (in the schools and from the pulpits)" (Kant 1979, 15). The crown is also entitled "not only to permit but even to require the faculties to let the government know, by their writings, everything they consider beneficial to a public religion of the land" (15). However, the government cannot presume to teach the faculties as to whether this or that tenet of religion is true. To exercise such censorship would be to mix revealed religion with the rational (natural) religion that is Kant's concern in *Religion Within the Limits of Reason Alone*. As a "purely philosophical" work on rational religion, his text has no reference to the Bible and Christianity, Kant scolds the king in turn; "and since I have always censured and warned against the mistake of straying beyond the limits of the science at hand or mixing one science with another, this is the last fault I could be reproached with" (15). As a philosopher of pure rational religion, Kant's answerability in matters of truth is, he says, solely to the commanding voice of reason:

> [I]t alone is the source of the *universality, unity,* and *necessity* in the tenets of faith that are the essence of any religion as such, which consists in the morally practical (in what we *ought* to do). On the other hand, what we have cause to believe on historical grounds (where "ought" does not hold at all)—that is, revelation as contingent tenets of faith—it regards as nonessential. (17)

With his distinction between rational religion and the revealed religion and between commands made by the voice of reason and those made by the king, Kant walls off scholarly judgments of truth from the civic domain and from the reach of government control. His distinction inscribes an inside/outside border around the university, what Derrida in "*Mochlos*" calls "a linear frontier, an indivisible and rigorously uncrossable line" (M 18). As Derrida points out, the line separates, and disallows the mixing of, two kinds of censorship: the one, *critique*, a critical judgement that gives no commands, answers only to truth, and is confined to the university's inside; the other, a political power that is backed by state force and that belongs in the public realm. The line is also, and at bottom, a division between two kinds of speech acts, "between one of truth and one of action, between one of theoretical statements and one of performatives (mostly commands) " (18). Kant constructs the entire university on the premise that this line can be drawn; he assumes that there is such a thing as a purely constative or theoretical language, and that the university is the place in which this language is housed. For its association with *visio* and the capacity to illuminate truth "before and in front of itself" (LIP 13), constative speech gives Kant's university a certain power of surveillance—the freedom to oversee and to censor in matters of truth, with such censoring supposedly untainted by technics or political power. When the philosophical institution speaks constatively, it does so, as it were, as the mouthpiece of the voice of reason, the voice that dictates its commands directly, without mediation, into the philosopher's ear.

Kant's inside/outside boundary is intended, in part, to withdraw this constative privilege to within the borders of the institution; his point is also to keep the performative language of gesture outside the university's walls. In *The Conflict*, gesture language is exercised most obviously through the voice of the state, as exemplified by the king's censoring letter to Kant. More broadly, however, gesture is characteristic of all language out in the world. As was the case two years before *The Conflict* in his 1796 satire, *Of An Overlordly Tone Recently Adopted in Philosophy*,[4] Kant wants to prevent any crossing of philosophy with performativity, with public discourse that, in all its heterogeneity, cannot be extricated from body and gesture, and that, because it is external to pure reason, does not speak with a unified and universal voice. Since public discourse deviates from the norm of philosophical address, it should not be allowed to mix with it, for the danger all such mixing poses, as Derrida notes in his reading of Kant's 1796 polemic, is the perversion of philosophy into *"mystagogy"*—into poetry, simulacrum, and mimicry (OAT 77). The public does not speak, nor on its own can it hear, the voice of pure reason: the public is full of incompetents—"idiots" [*Idioten*], Kant calls them—individuals whose ears are impenetrable to reason, either because they are too ignorant to listen or because they choose not to hear. How then, he asks the king, could *Religion Within the Limits of Reason Alone* do any harm to the public religion of the land? For "the book in question is not at all suitable for the public; to them it is an unintelligible, closed book, only a debate among scholars of the faculty, of which the people take no notice" (Kant 1979, 15).

Inasmuch as the border with which Kant encircles the university is supposed to withdraw the *logos*, logocentric speech, from contamination by body, gesture, mimicry, and the figurative language of *mythos*, it would bar from the university, even more than those who are too incompetent to listen, those whose ears cannot hear. Kant makes this clear in his *Anthropology From a Pragmatic Point of View*, the other of his last books, published the same year as *The Conflict*, at the moment when Kant's own senses were failing, a work in which he takes up the question of which sense loss is the most serious of all. What makes deafness a more profound deprivation than blindness, he explains in the *Anthropology*, is that this loss keeps one forever outside the *logos*, trapped in the language of gesture and mimicry. Sign language would be such mimicry, something that cannot be mixed with philosophy's tongue:

> If a deaf man was once able to hear, we can get him to speak as he used to by gesturing to him, and so by means of his eyes. He can also use his eyes to read our lips, or his sense of touch to feel our lip movements in the dark. If, however, he has been deaf from birth, his sense of *sight* must begin with movements of the vocal organs and convert the sounds he has been taught to make into a feeling of moving the muscles of his own vocal organs. But he never arrives at real concepts in this way, because the signs he uses are not the sort that can be universalized. (Kant 1974, 37)

In making this statement, Kant must have had more than his own senses in mind, for just at the time of his writing of the *Anthropology* and *The Conflict*, deafness became a matter of central concern in Europe, and the site around which, as Lennard Davis points out, a significant discourse was constructed. "Deafness as a phenomenon engaged the intellectual moment of this period in a way that blindness and other disabilities did not" (Davis 1995, 53). The reason for this is that "[d]eafness, after all, was about language," about lacking what, for the eighteenth century, was "the essential human quality of verbal communication" (53). Given that his relation to language was so "vexed" (53), the deaf person—the deaf ear and the mute mouth— became for Enlightenment culture a "point of fascination" (50) and an "icon" (51) of loss, a target against which rational subjectivity— and I would say, the rational university—was defined. For Kant, at least, the deaf person is an icon, an *os*, of this sort. For since, according to Kant, concepts are conveyed in words, since "words are the best means adapted to signifying concepts" (Kant 1974, 34), the man who is deaf from birth, and who must then "also remain dumb (without speech)," can never achieve more than a figure or simulacrum, "more than an analogue of reason" (34).

Derrida suggests in "*Mochlos*" that "[i]n tracing the system of the pure limits of the university, Kant wants to track any possible parasiting. He wants the power to exclude it—legitimately, legally" (M 15). Such exclusion would not be possible today. For example, one of the groups that Kant relegates to the outside of the university is made up of what he calls "businessmen or technicians of learning." These are university graduates who are employed by the government as ecclesiastics, magistrates, physicians, etc., and so who share in the government's exercise of political power. As tools of the crown, "instruments of the government, invested with an office for its own purpose (which is not exactly the progress of the sciences)" (Kant 1979, 25), the businessmen-technicians do not belong to the university, he says, and they must be prevented by law from usurping its power to judge: "[T]he government must keep them under strict control, to prevent them from trying to exercise judicial power, which belongs to the faculties" (25). In today's world, as Derrida points out, the label "businessmen or technicians of knowledge" would apply to "a massively larger variety and number of agents" who would be found on the university's inside as much as on its outside, including:

every responsible figure in the public or private administra-
tion of the university, every "decision-maker" in matters of
budgets and the allocation or distribution of resources (bu-
reaucrats in a ministry, "trustees," etc.), every administrator of
publications and archivization, every editor, journalist, etc. Is
it not, nowadays, for reasons involving the very structure of
knowledge, especially impossible to distinguish rigorously between scholars and technicians of science, just as it is to trace,
between knowledge and power, the limit within whose shelter
Kant sought to preserve the university edifice? (M 16)

Today, the university is no longer contained within the shelter
of Kant's border, but Derrida's argument in *"Mochlos"* is that the border was never intact. Right from the start, the modern university was
subject to parasiting, "menaced in certain places around its own body"
(M 15), and this for the reason that speech and language cannot be
divided along Kant's inside/outside line. In his very gesture of exclud-
ing the businessmen or technicians of learning, Kant had already
brought the outside in: and this is the quandry that inheres in the
theory/practice, constative/performative distinction.[5] The language of
saying is also, always, a language of doing: "For example—but one
could vary examples to infinity—the interpretation of a theorem, poem,
philosopheme or theologeme is only produced by simultaneously proposing an institutional model," and at the same time, "such a proposal
calls for the politics of an interpretive community gathered around
the text, and indeed of a global society with or without a state, a
veritable regime enabling the inscription of that community" (21). In
every "theoretical" operation we pursue, then, we should "acknowledge that an institutional concept is at play, a type of contract signed,
an image of the ideal seminar constructed, a *socius* implied, repeated
or displaced, invented, transformed, menaced or destroyed. An institution—that is not merely a few walls or some outer structure surrounding, protecting, guaranteeing or restricting the freedom of our
work; it is also and already the structure of our interpretation" (22).
Even on the threshold of *The Conflict of the Faculties*, Derrida
finds Kant's inside and outside to be "in excess of themselves" (M
26)—as if the university designed by *The Conflict* formed something
like a fold, "an *invaginated pocket*" (26). Moreover, as we cross the
threshold and move into the institution, we will not be done with

"this intestine division and its folding partition on the inside of each space" (26). Nor, as we move into the institution's interior, will we be done with the "extra-institutional" language of figures.

SECOND TURNING: IN THE FORM OF A COIL

Immediately on entering Kant's university (moving from the Preface to the Introduction to *The Conflict of the Faculties*), one encounters another territorial limit: *Religion Within the Limits of Reason Alone* cannot be censored by the king, Kant says, not just because, as a scholarly work, it belongs inside the university, but because it belongs inside the philosophy faculty. At the time of the writing of *The Conflict of the Faculties*, the university disciplines were organized into two ranks: three so-called "higher" faculties (law, medicine, theology) and one "lower" faculty (philosophy). Kant allows that this nomenclature is the work of the government, which labels the faculties of medicine, theology, and law as higher only because the function of these faculties is to train agents for the government itself: "Now the government is interested primarily in means for securing the strongest and most lasting influence on the people, and the subjects which the higher faculties teach are just such means" (Kant 1979, 27). By the same token, he adds, "the government reserves the right itself to *sanction* the teachings of the higher faculties, but those of the lower faculty it leaves up to the scholars' reason" (27). Here, Kant uses the less-than-perfect structure he inherits as something of a lever, offering the king this plan: the so-called higher faculties, because of what they teach, should be subject to political censorship, but the lower faculty, since it teaches only truth, must remain fully autonomous. With this distinction, Derrida observes, Kant extends the inside/outside barrier that circles the university so as to make it *coil* through the institution's inside, between the higher and lower faculties:

> Now this limit between reason that censors and reason foreign to censorship does not circumvent the university, but passes right through it, right between the two classes of faculties: the Higher Faculties (Theology, Law, Medicine), linked to the power of state they represent, and the Lower Faculty (Philosophy). No power should have the right of inspection over the Faculty of Philosophy, as long as it is

satisfied with *saying*, not *doing*; with saying the *truth* without giving *orders*, with speaking *within* the university and not *outside* of it. (LIP 128)

The external barrier that withdraws the scholar proper from the public, including the businessmen of learning, now winds like a spiral canal into the university's inside, where it separates the philosopher from the "businessmen-technicians" of the three higher faculties. The barrier marks off an internal space, the space of philosophy, as more interior, withdrawn closer to the center, than are the three higher faculties, and the barrier delimits this interior space of philosophy as the *place* where the language of reason is actually housed. The language of truth is now confined to this inner sphere, the narrowing shelter in which academic freedom would be safeguarded from government control. In Kant's university, only the lower faculty, philosophy, is fully autonomous, "independent of the government's command with regard to its teachings" and "free to evaluate everything" (Kant 1979, 27). The lower faculty "occupies itself with teachings which are not adopted as directives by order of a superior," Kant explains to the king, because "when it is a question of the *truth* of a certain teaching to be expounded in public, the teacher cannot appeal to a supreme command nor the pupil pretend that he believed it by order. This can happen only when it is a question of *action*" (43). It follows that "the philosophy faculty, because it must answer for the truth of the teachings it is to adopt or even allow, must be conceived of as free and subject only to laws given by reason, not by the government" (43).

Philosophy hears and answers solely to the voice of reason, not to political directives and not, Kant says, to all the pleas with which the public dogs the three higher faculties. "The people want to be *led*, that is (as demagogues say), they want to be *duped*," he complains (Kant 1979, 51). The people approach the scholars of the higher faculties "as if they were soothsayers and magicians"; they demand that the physicians, lawyers, and clergy of the higher faculties use their learning to deliver them undeserved health, wealth, and "an eleventh-hour ticket to heaven" (49). And the members of the higher faculties inevitably succumb to these demands: "the businessmen of the three higher faculties will always be such miracle-workers," Kant says, "unless the philosophy faculty is allowed to counteract them publicly—not in order to overthrow their teachings but only to deny the magic power that the public superstitiously attributes to these teachings and the rites connected with them" (51).

This matter of magic, and along with it, superstition, raptures, private revelations, sensuality, secrecy, equivocality: these are the disorders (the varying forms of "mystagogy") against which Kant inveighs in his 1796 tract *Of An Overlordly Tone Recently Adopted In Philosophy*. Now in *The Conflict*, his ire is raised again, for mystagogy, he says, is not just out in the city, it is inside the university's walls. Just as, for Kant in *Of an Overlordly Tone*, Plato the *academic* is also Plato the *letter writer*, so in *The Conflict*, Kant sees the mystagogue in his own fellow-scholar, the businessman-technician of the higher faculties. Once again, the problem is brought on by mixing or boundary crossing; the problem concerns a "confusion between two voices," here, "the voice of reason and the voice of the oracle" (OAT 70). Consider the supplementary reference in *The Conflict* to "[t]he fanaticism of *Postellus*, a sixteenth-century Venetian" who, Kant says, "serves as an excellent example of the sort of aberration, and indeed *logical* raving people can fall into if they transform the perceptible rendering of a pure idea of reason into the representation of an object of the senses" (Kant 1979, 67n). This is the risk that prompts Kant's withdrawal of philosophy from the three higher faculties—a separation that is also an elevation of the lower faculty over the others: the philosophy faculty must have "complete freedom" (53) to examine public teachings of the higher faculties, Kant contends, "for the lower faculty has not only the title but also the duty, if not to state the *whole* truth in public, at least to see to it that *everything* put forward in public as a principle is true" (53).

In every case, Kant's coiling margin is not only a theory/practice, philosophy/politics separation, but also a withdrawal of philosophy's voice from the sensory body and sensual figures—a gesture that makes for the institution's hierarchical and architectural elevation. This separation/elevation would distinguish the university's essence from its ornament. In *Of An Overlordly Tone Recently Adopted In Philosophy*, the ornament includes all the imagery and affective devices that decorate and obfuscate poetic language, and that are external, and inadmissible, to the language of reason. Similarly, in *Religion Within the Limits of Reason Alone*, the ornament, the *parergon*, is what supplements rational (natural) religion without belonging properly to it. Works of grace, miracles, mysteries, and means of grace are, Kant says, "*parerga* to religion within the limits of pure reason; they do not belong within it but border upon it" (Kant 1960, 47). *Parerga* are outside the sphere of rational religion, and the risk that they pose to it, the possibility of their crossing to the inside, is the risk of *fanaticism, superstition, illumination,* and *thaumaturgy*: "sheer aberrations of a reason going beyond its proper limits" (48; see also Kant 1979, 75). In *The Conflict of the Faculties*, the higher faculties are the *parerga* under discussion. These faculties border on philosophy, and are necessary as supplements to it, but the teachings of the higher faculties are not essential to what the university is about. "[A] university must have a faculty of philosophy," Kant writes. "Its function in relation to the three other faculties is to control them and, in this way, be useful to them, since *truth* (the essential and first condition of learning in general) is the main thing, whereas the *utility* the higher faculties promise the government is of secondary importance" (Kant 1979, 45).

The higher faculties are *parerga* to the shrinking university center. Something like the frame of a painting, the colonnades of palaces, or the clothing on statues, Kant's examples of *parerga* in his third *Critique*, the higher faculties are accessories that embellish the university body without being necessary to it; they are but sensible vehicles of university reason and of its "reason-to-be" (PR 3). Moreover, insofar as they are occupied with sensible, rather than supersensible, things, the higher faculties, like a gold frame that is introduced "merely to win approval for the picture by means of its charm" (Kant 1952, 68), can distract the university and tempt it to go astray.[6] Derrida points out in "Languages and Institutions of Philosophy" that, for Kant, it belongs to philosophy's *architectonic* function to keep the university on its proper path, true to its rational end. In *The Conflict of the Faculties*, Kant, the architect, takes on this architectonic task, the task he describes in his *Critique of Judgement* as involving a "critical examination of the ground" that is "carried down to the very depths of the foundations of the faculty of principles independent of experience, lest"—and this would seem to be the university's risk, poised as it is on the edge of an abyss—the entire edifice "give way, and, sinking, inevitably bring with it the ruin of all" (Kant 1952, 5).[7] Architectonics, which Kant (1966, 530) says is the art of constructing systems, would be what, by dividing the lower from the higher faculties, makes the university more than just a trade school, a school of businessmen or technicians of learning, held together by "know-how" as an aggregate of parts.[8] According to Kant, Derrida says, "[t]his 'know-how' [*savoir-faire*] fits together, without referring to principles, a multiplicity of contents in the contingent order in which they present themselves. One can always construct institutions according to technical schemas, with a concern for empirical profitability, without 'idea,' and without rational architectonics" (LIP 135). But a university without idea is dead, and this is the risk, the danger that the ornament poses (Kant 1979, 53).

For Kant, Derrida suggests, "[t]here is no university architecture without architectonics" (LIP 135). Architectonics organizes—and animates—the institution from the inside according to the principle of reason, and so makes the body a living, not merely a technical, whole. When Kant, the rational philosopher, engages architectonics in such texts as *The Conflict* and *The Critique of Pure Reason*, he does so by resorting to a language of figures, such as, Derrida notes in "Languages and Institutions," the figure of a living body, "the living organism as the totality of knowledge, of the natural seed out of which an academic institution develops" (134). This is a figure that Kant doubles—mixing philosophy with poetry, overlaying figure with figure—when he combines the metaphor of the living body with that of a well-made architectural structure, suggesting thereby that an architectonic institution is a "bioarchitectural totality, nature and artifact" (134) at once. Applied to the university, Kant's bioarchitectural figure could provide a model of the institutional balance that he wants to achieve: where the university would be constructed as a well-proportioned body, a body that, as in his footnote on the *hypomochlium*, is aligned on both its left and right feet—and so is able to push forward. The higher faculties are on the right side and the lower faculty is on the left, Kant says in *The Conflict*, using another double—biological and parliamentary—figure: "The rank of the higher faculties (as the right side of the parliament of learning) supports the government's statutes; but in as free a system of government as must exist when it is a question of truth, there must also be an opposition party (the left side), and this is the philosophy faculty's bench" (Kant 1979, 59). This right-left orientation is suggestive of the symmetry that Kant strives for in *The Conflict*. Both on the university's inside and in its relations with the state, his goal is "a system of regulated relationships," Derrida notes; "harmony, like a regulative idea, like an idea of reason, inspires all of the Kantian politics of the university"

(LIP 134). Yet the institution Kant designs is *not* balanced, and partly for the reason that he detaches the university's left side, the philosopher's speech, from its supporting figures, its skeletal *os*.

Kant excludes figurative language to philosophy's outside; yet even as he does so, he resorts to figures himself, and thereby takes the outside in, demonstrating that, as Derrida puts it in "Tympan," in a system of pure philosophy, the inside defines itself by delimiting its outside, but "*its* outside is never its *outside*" (MP xvi). For "to exclude something by placing it 'outside' is actually to control it, to put it in its place, to enclose it. To exclude is to include" (Wigley 1993, 127). To exclude is to internalize or consume: "Expulsion is consumption" (127). As we move farther into Kant's university, this intestine folding continues—to the point where what is being consumed is not just figurative language, but the figure, the sensible signifier, itself. It's at this point that the university, turned in on itself, becomes both deaf and mute.

THIRD TURNING: (AGAIN) THE FIGURE
OF THE CIRCLE (IN A CIRCLE)

Kant's discourse on the university suggests that the essence of the institution can be separated off from what is secondary and supplemental to it—that the *ergon* can be detached from the *parergon*—but the more tightly his margin coils around the space of pure reason, the more exteriority and corporeality it closes off, the more hierarchical, and less balanced, his institution becomes. For if, as Kant acknowledges himself (1979, 75), a *parergon* is necessary to supplement what is lacking in the interior, then its detachment would endanger the integrity and stability of the *ergon* itself. What for Kant constitutes *pererga*, Derrida says, "is not simply their exteriority as a surplus, it is the internal structural link which rivets them to the lack in the interior of the *ergon*. And this lack would be constitutive of the very unity of the *ergon*" (TP 59). Thus, Kant's efforts to dissociate the inside from the outside, and the lower from the higher faculties, can only leave the university with a structural problem—as becomes quite evident when we follow him into the university center where his coiling margin turns another circle and draws another inside/ outside line. This line extends the barrier between the university and the world, and between the lower and the higher faculties, so as to partition the lower faculty itself. The philosophy faculty must be divided into two separate departments, Kant says:

> a department of *historical knowledge* (including history, geography, philology and the humanities, along with all the empirical knowledge contained in the natural sciences), and a department of *pure rational knowledge* (pure mathematics and pure philosophy, the metaphysics of nature and of morals). And it also studies the relation of these two divisions of learning to each other. It therefore extends to all parts of human knowledge (including, from a historical viewpoint, the teachings of the higher faculties), though there are some parts (namely, the distinctive teachings and precepts of the higher faculties) which it does not treat as its own content, but as objects it will examine and criticize for the benefit of the sciences. (Kant 1979, 45)

This partitioning of the lower faculty now confines university autonomy to the department of pure rational knowledge, and to the philosopher of pure reason. And the partitioning makes another, final, withdrawal of the inner place of pure reason from the outer world, and from the encasing of all worldly, scientific, and historical knowledge. This rational interior must be completely nonempirical, Kant explains—and yet, in stating his case, he cannot achieve more than a figure or analogue of reason. In *Religion Within the Limits of Reason Alone*, for instance, Kant proposes a topological figure that, Derrida says, "prefigures or configures" (LIP 131) the location of rational philosophy in the research university. The figure, if not a coil, is of two concentric circles, one inside the other. Kant maintains that "[t]he philosopher, as a teacher of pure reason (from unassisted principles *a priori*), must confine himself within the narrower circle, and, in so doing, must waive consideration of all experience" (Kant 1960, 11).

From within this innermost circle, the pure rational philosopher enjoys "panoptical ubiquity" (LIP 132) at the very top of the university; he has a view of, and right of inspection over, all of the faculties, "is able to comprehend in his vision and his critical inspection the entire field of knowledge" (132). This placement of pure philosophy at the pinnacle of Kant's hierarchical university may well be consistent with the elevation in all of Western metaphysics of theoretical (or philosophical) over practical knowledge: Derrida suggests as much, noting that Aristotle described the theoretician as an architect and singled him out as a teacher and leader of men, "the leader or *arkhitekton* of a society at work," who, by virtue of his knowledge of causes and principles, "is positioned above the manual laborer [*kheiroteknes*] who acts without knowing" (PR 18).[9] Derrida also notes, however, that the theory/practice, philosophy/politics hierarchy takes on a new significance with Kant, for it is right around the time of *The Conflict* that the philosopher first becomes a civil servant of the state, "a '*Dozent*,' someone who teaches disciples and whose qualifications are legitimized by the state. He has a certain status, which is not the status that dominated philosophy before Kant" (LIP 132). It is important to note that in this new situation of the "state institutionalizing of reason, a 'facultization' of reason" (132), Kant secures pure reason's privilege at the institution's top *by way of subordinating space*—and then collapsing it altogether. The pure philosopher's ocular vantage point is, then, no more than that: "his space is reduced to almost nothing—just a point" (OCP 211). No room here for a philosopher-in-the-flesh: now a "sublime body" (LIP 138), Kant's master of pure reason "haunts " (138) the modern university.

Just how he haunts the institution depends on the nature of the "oblique and indirect relationship" (CM 207) that Derrida says exists between *The Conflict of the Faculties* and Heidegger's Rectorate Address. I take this relationship to concern the gathering that goes on in both texts: a Medusa effect recoil from the other-outside, which at the same time, as a gathering close-to-self, subordinates spacing. In *The Conflict*, this withdrawal/self-proximity is, on both of its sides, about hearing: it withdraws reason from its figure of loss and privileges pure audiblity. More than the privilege accorded to sight, it is the priority (proximity) of the pure philosopher's hearing that puts him at the university's top, where space is altogether collapsed into a nonempirical inside. The voice of reason speaks equally to all, Kant says, but the pure rational philosopher, because he claims to be self-present, fully interiorized, is supposed to hear reason's voice before and better than others. He is supposed to hear reason speak (in words) *immediately*, that is, before there has been any movement to the outside, and before a material signifier, a figure, has intervened. The pure philosopher hears before he needs physical ears, and from within a pure interior where his hearing organs are, in any case, cut off—disembodied. The gesture of their detachment is, I suggest, *The Conflict's* most politically charged moment. Here, the haunting starts. For Kant's final withdrawal of human essence into a transcendent ideal looks forward to Heidegger's similar gathering of essence into spirit in the Rectorate Address—Heidegger, gathering spirit away from what he calls a deaf-and-dumb animal *os*, Kant drawing the idea back from those who, because they have never heard reason speak, have to stay outside the university's walls. Not incidentally, it is from within the pure interior, from his point at the institution's top, that Kant dreams ahead to the day when the lower faculty, the place where truth resides, will be made high, that is, will be called upon to guide the ruler's power:

> [I]t could well happen that the last would some day be first (the lower faculty would be the higher)—not, indeed, in authority, but in counseling the authority (the government). For the government may find the freedom of the philosophy faculty, and the increased insight gained from this freedom, a better means for achieving its ends than its own absolute authority. (Kant 1979, 59)[10]

There are, Derrida emphasizes, many profound differences between *The Conflict* and the Rectorate Address. What is more, Kant would have judged the Rectorate Address and all that it implies as "scandalous" (CM 208). For Heidegger's Address "transgresses every rule imposed by *The Conflict of the Faculties.* The concept of truth it propounds is no longer the same. The reference to a singular people and to the German character of the university, the privilege accorded the German language in the *Introduction to Metaphysics* of 1935 (which, on this point, is closer to Hegel), the rather disdainful allusions to a certain concept of academic freedom, all this is not only not very compatible with the spirit of *The Conflict of the Faculties,* but with the pacifist and cosmopolitan spirit of a certain *Aufklärung* that animates it. And there would be further complications, further nuances" (208). Even as he makes this point, however, Derrida also notes that there are "some Kantian elements" (207) in the Rectorate Address, not the least of which has to do with Kant's dream that one day the philosopher, without exercising power, will inspire it. "Did not Heidegger also dream of playing this paradoxical role during the Rectorate?" (208). The dream that Kant and Heidegger have in common presupposes a distinction between the language of saying and the language of doing, and so calls into question all of the inside/outside boundaries that Kant builds into his university blueprint. In *The Conflict*, I have suggested, all of these either/or divisions come to rest on the absolute separation (and elevation) of the philosopher's sublime ear from its externalized deaf other.

MOCHLOS OS

> A university is always the construction of a philosophy
>
> —Derrida, *Who's Afraid of Philosophy?*

Deconstruction, Derrida says, is not just a matter of written texts, but also of passage through solid structures: it "goes *through* certain social and political structures, meeting with resistance and displacing institutions as it does" (JD 72). I take his reading of *The Conflict* to be "deconstructive," then, by way of its open and munching mouth, the "*Mochlos*" *os*. This mouth, moving and materialized, replaces the *os mutum* and its fantasy of female loss. Chewing holes in Kant's devouring university margin so as to let the voice pass through and out, this mouth, this hybrid "*Mochlos*" *os*, is empty of either/or, male/female dichotomies; a figure of excess, it inscribes the crossing of fixed us/them and inside/outside boundaries. As such a figure, the "*Mochlos*" *os* says something about university responsibility. "[A]n essential surplus or excess of responsibility is somehow the 'normal' condition of responsibility," Derrida suggests. "If it were not excessive, if it could assign limits to itself, appease itself, arrest itself or calculate its own proportions, then the meaning claimed for 'responsibilities' would include anything but the meaning of responsibility. It would confuse responsibility with a calculation of causalities and programs. Responsibility is infinite or it is not"(CM 203).

In *The Conflict*, the figure of the *os* as mouth (or as *oris*, perforation) is inseparable from the *os* as *hypomochlium*, organ of hearing and balance. At the close of his "Mochlos," Derrida links the latter *os* to another late work of Kant's, the 1786 essay *What Is Orientation In Thinking? (Was heisst: Sich im Denken orientieren?)*. In this text, Kant explains that the division of right from left originates not from a rational concept but from a *subjective* distinction, "the feeling of difference between my two sides, my right and my left" (Kant 1970, 239). Kant's statement makes for another conflict, or crossing, at the university's very interior, where the rational philosopher is authorized to divide the left from the right sides of the institutional body. This all-important, architectonic, difference does not derive from "a conceptual or logical determination, but rather from a sensory topology" (M 31), Kant here (in *What Is Orientation?*) concedes. With such *mythos-logos* mixing, we might say, he has already opened the university's borders. Kant himself has suggested how we might push forward from here.

THREE

PASSAGES

An *after*-effect [*un effet d*'après] offers endless resistance there.

—Derrida, *Glas*

REBOUND

The works of Egyptian art in their mysterious symbolism are therefore riddles; the objective riddle *par excellence*. As a symbol for this proper meaning of the Egyptian spirit we may mention the Sphinx. It is, as it were, the symbol of the symbolic itself. In innumerable quantities, set up in rows in hundreds, there are sphinx shapes in Egypt, constructed out of the hardest stone, polished, covered with hieroglyphics, and [one] near Cairo is of such colossal size that the lion's claws alone amount to a man's height. Some of them are recumbent animal bodies out of which an upper part, the human body, struggles; here and there again there is a ram's head, but elsewhere most commonly a female head. Out of the dull strength and power of the animal the human spirit tries to push itself forward, without coming to a perfect portrayal of its own freedom and animated shape, because it must still remain confused and associated with what is other than itself.

—Hegel, *Aesthetics: Lectures on Fine Art*

SINCE WE ARE CONCERNED in this chapter with Hegel, we have to begin in the East. In the dawnlight, where the sun of world history first rises. We have to begin in the East, for as Hegel has it, "the course of History, the great Day's work of Spirit," follows the sun from East to West, from the Orient ("Here rises the outward physical Sun,

47

and in the West it sinks down") to the Occident (where "by the close of the day man has erected a building constructed from his own inner Sun") (Hegel 1991a, 103). Because spirit's historical journey gives us the meaning of freedom ("the essence of Spirit is Freedom" [17]) and the story of its progress through the institutions of the world, the university among them, we have to open with this solar course, make our start where Hegel's grand narrative begins.

Like Kant, Hegel equates freedom with proximity to self: the will is free only when it is, as he puts it, "completely *with itself* [*bei sich*]," only when it has reference to "nothing but itself" (Hegel 1991b, 54 §23). For Hegel, however, as distinct from Kant, freedom is attained not by withdrawal from the world but by way of *passage* through it, a process of overcoming that integrates the other into *being-for-self*. Pure light, pure idea, is a mere abstraction; it manifests nothing, Hegel says. For history's (freedom's) unfolding to commence, spirit, with all the energy that propels its externalizing movement, must submerge itself in the otherness of matter, from within which, in the (East-to-West) process of returning to (the concept of) itself, it will then agitate for release. Spirit, we might say, is the sound source. To achieve its result, resonance with itself and for itself, spirit must, for a start, *strike upon* a hard object, a solid body, something dark, as Hegel puts it a footnote to his *Lectures on the Philosophy of Religion* (Hegel 1988, 303 n281). As if audibility required externality, "the other" he refers to in the footnote—as if, as I am arguing in this book, there can be no hearing without an outside, without an imprint, without writing of some sort—Hegel's grand narrative begins by opening silence to the spacing movement of a stroke. At the beginning, however, when it strikes a hard object such as stone, spirit "produces only a noise, not a sonorous vibration, since the shock, though propagated, does not return to itself" (Hegel 1970, 141). When the return to (resonance with) itself is achieved with the closing of the solar circle in the West, the stroke will be stopped, and the imprint, the signifier, will be absorbed into absolute spirit or absolute knowledge (which in *Glas* becomes *savoir absolu*, Derrida's siglum for which is *Sa*). Few can doubt "the strange privilege of sound" in Hegel's system, in the process of "idealization, the production of the concept and the self-presence of the subject" (OG 12). And yet, as I will argue in this chapter, *Sa* is *silence absolute*. As much as in Kant—and despite all the difference that he says his system has from Kant's—Hegel's *Sa* is a Medusa effect that cuts off both tongue and ear. His grand narrative ends where it begins, in stillness, silence, and with the signifier consumed. This may serve only to show us, to use Hegel's words, that a "circle is the line returning into itself" (Hegel 1970, 70).

We can begin in Egypt, in the darkness of the Egyptian desert, where spirit, which has already coursed through China and India, finds in the Sphinx a hard object to strike. An oscillation, some manifestation of freedom, begins to be felt here, although at this stage, history's tympan, *so hard it is*, vibrates with merely a tremor: how could it be otherwise, Hegel seems to ask, as he dwells on the enormity, the "most stupendous size," of the Sphinx, and its rigidity, carved in massive stone, sitting at stolid attention. One Sphinx in Cairo, he says, "is 148 feet long, the height from the claws to the head is 65 feet, the feet extended in front are 57 feet from the breast to the point of the claws, and the claws are 8 feet high" (Hegel 1975 II, 643). The prodigious size defies all human proportion—which is why the Sphinx *cannot speak*, remains all but mute, when entered by spirit: we have not yet progressed to Greece, where statues, although they are still made of stone, correspond to the upright, hence human, form and so *hear*—receive and resound more fully with—the free light of spirit. "The figure has not yet risen to be a free and a beautiful one, it is not yet spiritualized to clarity" (Hegel 1988, 325–26). Hence the enigmatic expression the Sphinx wears on her face: the Egyptian moment is *daimonic*, a moment of transition, of confusion and boundary crossing, when spirit has yet to disengage itself from the otherness of animal nature and find its own image in man:

> Of the representations which Egyptian Antiquity presents us with, one figure must be especially noticed, viz. *the Sphinx*— in itself a riddle—an ambiguous form, half brute, half human. The Sphinx may be regarded as a symbol of the Egyptian Spirit. The human head looking out from the brute body exhibits Spirit as it begins to emerge from the merely Natural—to tear itself loose therefrom and already to look more freely around it; without, however, entirely freeing itself from the fetters Nature had imposed. (Hegel 1991a, 199)

That the stone deaf, and mute, face of the hybrid Sphinx is "most commonly" (Hegel 1975 I, 361) that of a woman (a "virgin"

[Hegel 1991a, 213]), is in keeping with Egypt's status as transitional, a mediating moment. With its innumerable hieroglyphic symbols—the Sphinxes, Memnons, and Pyramids—half above ground and half below, the whole of Egypt, Hegel says, is divided into a realm of light and a realm of darkness, "into a kingdom of life and a kingdom of death" (Hegel 1991a, 199).[1] In that its script is hieroglyphic and not phonetic, based on "only the sensuous image, not the letter itself" (199), Egypt also remains, in its language, a subterranean world, dumb to signification, to spirit's inner life; however, insofar as its hieroglyphs are partially phonetic, they indicate that the passage to Greek and German is underway, mediated by the Egyptian phase. It's as if, in this early externalization, spirit had, as it were, already come back home to itself; as if the middle already disappeared into the joining of beginning and end, for as Hegel puts it himself, "the first traces of Spirit virtually contain the whole of that History" (Hegel 1991a, 18). Considering the inscription of the temple of the goddess Neith in Lower Egypt, then, Hegel, in his *Philosophy of Religion* (1988, 326–27), "deciphers it in Greek-German in order to read in it the whole course of the sun setting in the West and recalling itself within itself" (G 256a).

This history of spirit, as Derrida argues in *Glas* and as I consider more fully below, "is a family history" (G 256a)—and that is why the Sphinx so appropriately bears a woman's (a Medusa's) head. In Hegel's system, the fate of the woman parallels that of the Sphinx: both are hybrid creatures, belonging part to darkness and part to light; both are inactive, bound to the earth, weighed down by sensuous matter, and in need of light from without; in short, both lack the capacity for speech that starts from, and resonates with, *hears*, itself first. The Sphinx and the woman, then, are mediators only. Precisely because, with them, sound and hearing depend on exteriority, these middles must be made to disappear. This disappearance of the middle—a *passage*, an *Aufhebung*—is the Hegelian version of what I am calling the Medusa effect. What, for Hegel, is "speechless," what lacks the self-resonance that ideal speech and hearing entail, is what remains other, its voice not interiorized. It is the woman in particular who represents this deaf and mute *os*, figure of the middle (figure, I will suggest later, of the *voice of the other*), in Hegel's familial philosophy, in this philosophy of spirit that has a family structure. In the next section, I turn to the concept of the family in Hegel, and to the "familial" structure of passage and of history-as-passage that, as Derrida says in *Glas*, Hegel's system is: where end joins beginning through the "relief" (from *relever*), the "relief [*relève*] of naturalness" (G 15a), and where the woman, like the Sphinx, is a natural-middle that disappears.[2] We can approach Hegel's university only by way of this family scene.

ALMA MATER

> Women may well be educated, but they are not made for the higher sciences, for philosophy and certain artistic productions which require a universal element. Women may have insights [*Einfälle*], taste, and delicacy, but they do not possess the ideal.

> —Hegel, *Elements of the Philosophy of Right*

To move from Kant's university to Hegel's requires a passage through the family. For it is the family that Hegel inserts between Kant's concept of freedom and his own. Hegel inserts the family, in the first place, as a determinate moment, what in his *Elements of the Philosophy of Right* he describes as the first moment of *Sittlichkeit*,[3] where freedom, beyond the abstract formulation that he says it has in Kant, begins to work through the institutions of the world. The family, first of *Sittlichkeit*'s three moments (family, civil society, state), is in turn a syllogism comprised of three moments: marriage, property, education of children. Since *Sittlichkeit* itself is the third moment of another syllogism (abstract right, morality [*Moralität*], *Sittlichkeit*), the family, as the first stage of *Sittlichkeit*, mediates the passage from abstract to actual freedom. In *Sittlichkeit*, Derrida says, "the [Kantian] Idea of freedom becomes actually present, is no longer only in the head of subjective individuals" (G 11a). And because the family is a moment of *Sittlichkeit*, though its first and most natural stage, it belongs to ethical life, and must be recognized as an institution of freedom. Hegel wants us to think of marriage this way: while the family's first and most natural moment, marriage still belongs to rational and ethical life of *Sittlichkeit*, not to sexual or animal nature. "There is no love nor family in physical or biological nature. *Logos*, reason, freedom are love's milieu" (G 12a). Marriage enables the leap to be made from animal to human nature, for it produces children who will go on to become free rational selves. Education, third and final stage of the family, the moment that brings the family circle to a close, enables this passage into free rational subjectivity, citizenship, and *Sittlichkeit*'s highest moment, the nation-state. Education, by constituting the nation, thus extends the family beyond the confines of the hearth. "Animal copulation leaves behind itself no monument, no burial place, no institution, no law that opens and assures any history. It names nothing" (G 12a). But the human, rational family, when it ceases to exist as a particular entity, *goes on* through the education of children into the higher stages of *Sittlichkeit*, into rational citizenship and the ethical life of the people (*Volksgeist*); and through death, into the universality of spirit.

We can't get to Hegel's university without a passage through the family, and this is one of the reasons why Derrida takes us through the family in *Glas*—through its first moment, marriage, which produces children who, through its third moment, education, go on to become free, spiritual, selves. Derrida is interested in Hegel's family, however, not only as a determinate moment, but also as this moment's trinitarian schema or structure. The structure is already evident in the relieving union of opposites that Hegelian marriage is, where the wife, drawn up into the light by her husband's seed, falls back and disappears in the movement that sets his spirit free in a son. "The union of opposites, of man and woman, has the form of a syllogistic copulation" (G 170a). The "copulative" structure, and with it, Hegel's opposition of the sexes, is put in place again with the transition to higher education. Education is a family relief: in bringing the family circle to a close, it accomplishes the family's end (the loss of itself as nature, the regaining of itself as spirit). Education, as Derrida puts it, is "a constituting/deconstituting process of the family, an *Aufhebung* by which the family accomplishes itself, *raises itself* in destroying itself or falling (to the tomb) as family" (G 13a). But since, according to Hegel, only sons go on beyond the home to higher education, since only sons are expelled from the womb and passed on to their alma mater, in this *Aufhebung* of the family, it is the woman, and only the woman, who falls back—to the tomb—as an after-birth that eventually decays and disappears, animal matter to be consumed.[4] In the meantime, in the son's classroom, *in loco parentis*, higher education repeats the family schema, returning the father to himself in the rearing (raising) of his son.[5] "The relieving education interiorizes the father" (G 133a).

The family, more than a moment, is a structure—"his propositions are structural" (G 165a)—and the *oikos*, economy of the house, is the structure of passage itself. "The *Aufhebung*, the economic law of absolute reappropriation of the absolute loss, is a family concept" (G 133a). This means that the family is put back in place each time a syllogistic circle closes, with each passage of spirit through history: "The whole system repeats itself in the family" (G 20a). This means also that the family, Christianity's Holy Family, provides an overarching structure for history, history-as-passage to the concept. It is because Christianity—where God becomes father and where a trinitarian schema of return-to-self is established—is a religion of the family that Hegel privileges it as *the* religion of spirit. Christianity makes of spirit's return-journey through history an absolute Holy Family scene, something that Judaism—a kind of Kantianism where God remains abstract, does not become a father ("A father without a son is not a father" [G 31a])—could never do. Thus, Hegel interprets the passage from Judaism to Christianity (and from Kant's philosophy to his own) as a passage to the family, "as the advent of love, in other words, of the family as the relief of formal and abstract morality (*Moralität*) (in that respect Kantianism is, structurally, a Judaism)" (G 33a–34a). At the same time, however, since his system is a system of circles, "spiral chaining of the circle of circles" (G 245a), Hegel puts the family in place at the start, before the family-as-family arrives.[6] We already find the family schema at the beginning, in the East, for instance, in primitive pantheistic nature worship, in the religion of the flower. "First passage: religion of flowers" (G 2a). In the syllogism of natural religion (religion of the sun, religion of plants [flowers] and animals, religion of the artificer), the flower, prefiguring the role of woman in the family, mediates the movement of sun (spirit) into the animal. "The innocence of the *flower religion*, which is merely the self-less idea of self, gives way to the earnestness of warring life, to the guilt of animal religions," Hegel writes (1977, 420). The "passivity and impotence" of the flower, "the innocent indifference of plant life," gives way to being-for-self (420). In the syllogism of natural religion, the flower "is not even a moment or station," Derrida observes. "It all but exhausts itself in a passage (*Übergehen*), a disappearing movement, the effluvium floating above the procession, the march from innocence to guilt" (G 2a).

Every Hegelian passage (*Übergehen*: *über* = over, across + *gehen* = go) puts the family's copulative structure back in place, and with that, reinstates the two opposing laws to which, he says, the sexes belong. The man's law "is the law of *day(light)* because it is known, public, visible, *universal*; human law rules, not the family, but the *city*, government, war, and it is made by *man (vir)*" (G 142a). To the man belong consciousness and the ongoing life of the people-spirit; to the woman belongs unconsciousness, "the economy of the dead, the law of the *oikos* (tomb)" (G, 142a). Her law "hides itself, does not offer itself in this opening-manifestation (*Offenbarkeit*) that produces man" (G 142a); her law is "nocturnal and more natural than the law of universality, just as the family is more natural than the city" (G 142a). While the son goes on beyond the family, then, the daughter remains behind—as remains—preparing to become a wife; her role is to tend to the toilette of the dead, to busy herself around the man's burial place: she mourns him, shrouds and buries his corpse, engraves his tomb, preserves his archive, ensures his monumentalization.[7] Impotent to raise herself beyond the most natural moment of *Sittlichkeit*, incapable of passing into universality herself, the woman appears only to disappear. In Hegel's familial schema of passage, she mediates the return of spirit to spirit—she is "the middle (*Mitte*), the means by which the spirit emerges from its inactuality, passes from the unconscious to the conscious" (G 170a)—but each time the family circle closes, the woman, the middle, is crossed out.[8] In what follows, I consider how, with this crossing out of the middle—the speechless, impotent, woman—Hegel's dialectical philosophy becomes what Derrida calls a *dialectophagy* (G 9a) that, in order to *hear-itself-speak*, swallows its own tongue.[9]

STONE DEAF

> When a body sounds, we feel we are entering a higher sphere; sound affects our innermost feeling. It speaks to the inner soul since it is itself inner and subjective. Sound, by itself, is the self of the individuality, not an abstract ideal. . . . Now if we ask with reference to sound as such why it is connected with hearing, we must answer that it is because this sense belongs to the mechanical sphere and is moreover the sense connected with the flight from materiality, with the transition from the material to the ideal.
>
> —Hegel, *Philosophy of Nature*

What would make of the flower a Sphinx—if not a mute *os*, the incapacity for speech that, according to Hegel, characterizes both of these middles and makes them apt figures of the other sex? Muteness belongs to the law of the woman, so much so, that all of Hegel's binary oppositions—darkness and light, passivity and activity, closed and open, unconscious and conscious, death and life—come to rest on the opposition of silence and speech. We see this in the plant (flower) that he dwells on at length in his *Philosophy of Nature*, and that he opposes to the animal, in much the same way that, in his discussion of the family, he opposes woman to man. Indeed, since, according to Hegel, "[t]he difference between man and woman is the difference between animal and plant; the animal is closer in character to man, the plant to woman" (Hegel 1991b, 207), we might look to the *Philosophy of Nature* for a description of the difference between the family's male and female—as well as for an instance of (the familial) passage as *passage into voice*, into "the reverberating interiority couple that voice and hearing form" (G 250a). For at every point in his discussion of the animal and plant, Hegel poses the difference between them as the difference between what possesses, and what lacks, a voice. "Voice," he says, "is the high privilege of the animal, which can appear wonderful; it is the utterance of sensation, of self-feeling. The animal makes manifest that it is inwardly for-itself, and this manifestation is voice" (Hegel 1970, 354). Voice is the hallmark of the free selfhood or subjectivity that is lacking in the plant. "The plant is still not veritable subjectivity," he emphasizes (276). The plant "is not yet a self-subsistent subjectivity" (305); it does not exist "as something subjective" (308). Its impotence is the "impotence of self-relation" (276), for the plant does not return to itself in the bud, does not, as does a self, have "a relation to itself" (308); "its individuality always falls apart into its particularity, and so does not hold on to itself as an infinite being-for-self" (308). And the plant is not self-active; it has no freedom of self-movement, cannot "freely determine its place, i. e. *move from the spot*" (305). Like the subterranean abodes that are symbols of Egypt, those enormous excavations in the hills along the Nile, like the Sphinx in all its heavy matter, the plant, the flower, cannot free itself from the earth, cannot loose itself from the woman's law of darkness and the underground. This is why Hegel says that in the passage from the plant to the animal, "heaviness is first truly overcome" (352). This passage, from plant to animal, is the passage from silence to voice:

> The animal has freedom of *self-movement* because its subjectivity is, like light, ideality freed from gravity, a free time

which, as removed from real externality, *spontaneously determines its place*. Bound up with this is the animal's possession of a *voice*, for its *subjectivity* as *real* ideality (soul), dominates the abstract ideality of time and space and displays its self-movement as a free vibration *within itself* (353).

In establishing the difference between the animal and the plant, as analogous to the difference between the sexes, it is important for Hegel to note that the plant remains dependent on an outside self, on man's law, on light: "It is in light that all the plant's energies develop, and it acquires scent and colour; it is light that endows the plant with these qualities, and also holds it upright" (338).[10] The passage into voice thus marks the difference between what, like the flower, requires stimulation from the outside and *thereby entails spatialization*, and what vibrates within and close to itself, displaying in this self-proximity a kind of "elasticity of inner being" (139). All of Hegel's East-to-West history of spirit is about this difference between exterior and interior sound, the difference between nature and spirit as "the difference between what does not resonate starting from (it)self" and "what resonates with (it)self" (G 249a). While "[m]etals have sound," then, as he notes in his *Philosophy of Nature*, "this still is not voice; voice is the spiritualized mechanism which thus utters itself. The inorganic does not show its specific quality until it is stimulated from outside, gets struck; but the animal sounds of its own accord" (Hegel 1970, 354). As Hegel explains in his *Aesthetics* (1975 II, 642–48), the prime instance of such noise-not-yet-become-voice is found, of course, in Egypt, in the huge Memnon statues at Thebes that produce sound when warmed by the morning sun. The vibrating Memnons demonstrate the direct relation that exists between sound and heat; and as Derrida notes, in producing a sound (*Klang*) when entered by the sun, they set up a structural correspondence with the family, and with the passage that the family is:

Correspondences: the moment immediately following both the flower religion and the phallic columns, a moment that relieves them forthwith as it were, is Memnon, the resonating colossal statue (*kolossale Klangstatue*) that produces a *Klang* under the incidence of the sun's rays. The *Klang* announces the end of the flower religion and the phallic columns, but is not yet voice or language. This ringing, sonorous light reverberating as on a stone bell [*cloche*] is already no longer mute, but not yet speaking (*nur Klang und nicht Sprache*). These structural correspondences can be verified among all the descriptions of *Klang* in the *Aesthetics*, the *Phenomenology of Spirit*, the *Philosophy of Nature*, etc. (G 3ai)

In Egypt, as symbolized by the Memnons, language remains hieroglyphic, *nonphonetic*, thus "insufficiently filled with signification" (G 251a). The limit of the Egyptian stage of history results also from "a spatialization of language," marked in the fact that, here, "sound remains exterior, produced by light, the moment the sun's ray comes to strike the stone" (G 251a). With the passage from sound into voice, "animal heat" (Hegel 1970, 355) begins to generate the self's own interior vibrations—in the movement of a closed circle that starts from, and returns into, itself (355). This progress in the communion of the self with itself makes yet another leap in the passage from voice into speech: feeling, Hegel says, "feeling of universality is the highest to which the animal can attain" (412), but when, with the passage to the family, voice gives way to speech, feeling rises to thought. All of history advances to this destination, the joining of phonetic speech and thought, a process that begins in Asia and that reaches its "absolute end" in Europe (Hegel 1991a, 103), in Hegel's own German, the "naturally speculative tongue" (G 32a). From this, the most spiritual and familial of all languages, we pass to Hegel's *Sa*, a kind of immaculate conception that, in crossing out the middle term, eats the body (of language) altogether. *Sa* is "[t]he *Aufhebung* of natural exteriority, the *relève* of the visible into the audible" (MP 93), an idealized instance that, as I have been arguing, deafens. *Sa*, then, is mute; pure interiority, *silence absolute*. I turn now to Derrida's attempt to re-embody the ear in *Glas*. We have to begin again with the family.

A LEGEND

So one must interrogate this circular and teleological structure of the before and after, this speculative reading of the future perfect that puts the family before itself.

—Derrida, Glas

> Discursive utterances about closure are necessary, but they are insufficient if one seeks to deform closure, as well as displace it. Not just this or that but the form "closure," the enclosing structure.
>
> —Derrida, "Between Brackets I," in *Points*

> A sensible remain(s) prevents the three-stroke engine from turning over or running smoothly.
>
> —Derrida, *Glas*

As far as genre is concerned, *Glas* is a mutant. It's a *daimon*-work that does not conform to the academic standards of either a philosophical or a literary text. Two words that Derrida has used to describe the book are "hybrid" and "monster" (DO 122–23). Translator John P. Leavey Jr. calls it "a strange text. A square text. Upon opening it, you see an odd typography. At least two separate columns confront you, columns erected impassively one against the other, in architectural terms, distyle" (Leavey 1986, 32c). In keeping with philosophy's left-bench placement in the modern university, *Glas* deals with philosophy, *logos*, in its left column and literature, *mythos* (what Kant would surely call *mystagogy*), in its right. And yet, Derrida says, the book "is neither philosophy nor poetry. It is in fact a reciprocal contamination of the one by the other, from which neither can emerge intact" (DO 122). Internally, each column of *Glas* combines diverse modes and styles of writing and even typefaces; and each is tattooed with what Derrida calls "judas" pockets, cut open by these incisions and by insertions such as: etymologies, some of which go on for pages; citations from philosophical and literary works; many excerpts from letters, the *Letters* of Hegel included; and various and diverse "bits and pieces" of other texts. Gregory Ulmer calls *Glas* an "experiment in a new academic writing" (Ulmer 1986, 23b). John Leavey asks: "Can it be read?" (Leavey 1986, 32a).

I take *Glas* to be a work on the family. In order to approach Hegel's signature, *Sa*, in order to countersign the Hegelian text, Derrida must deal with the family. The family, he writes in the left column, is the "one thread" on which he chooses to draw: "It is the law of the family: of Hegel's family, of the family in Hegel, of the concept family according to Hegel" (G 4a). Given that, as Derrida informs us at the opening of the Hegel column, *Glas* is a legend ("This is—a legend" [G 1a]), I take the book to be not only a discourse on the family but also, in its layout, a family rebus. Gayatri Spivak notes that while a fable is spoken, a legend (L *legere*: to read; *legendus*: fit or needing to be read) has to be read: the *Glas* legend, which, through the root *legein*, "turns *logos* into writing," must be read, she says, "not merely as a story or argument but as a significant typographical design" (Spivak 1977, 25). With this in mind, I read the two columns of *Glas* as the layout of Hegel's familial and pedagogical structure: on the left, Hegel, the philosophical father; on the right, Genet, the poet who takes on his mother's name; and between these two, the father and the mother, Derrida, who, in Spivak's words, attempts "to place the son's (his own) signature" (23) as the family's middle term. Read this way, as a familial structure, the design of *Glas* sets up the fantasy of loss I have been tracking in this book. For as Freud explains in "Medusa's Head," "Fetishism," and other essays, a son, positioned between his father and his mother, can only be struck with terror at the threat of castration: "Probably no male human being is spared the fright of castration at the sight of a female genital" (Freud [1927] 1961, 154).[11] I have been arguing thus far in this book that the male's dread fear of losing the member he perceives his mother (Medusa) to lack is actually an aural-oral trauma. This is certainly the case in Hegel, where seed or semen is assimilated to speech, is "the ontotheological figure of the family" (G 27a), and where virility is tied to inner speech as active hearing.[12] Fear of the mute mouth and the deaf ear is what makes Hegel stiffen erect, *raising* the male beyond the family into higher education, while the woman, as impotent *os*, is crossed out and let fall into the tomb. In the middle, between the two legs of *Glas*, as the figure—and the writing, the signifier—that would disappear, Derrida's work of resistance to this fantasy is done.

For one thing, *Glas* resists, thwarts, the "circular pedagogy" (G 15ai) that Hegel's familial schema is. Legend relates to *lexie*, dialectics, and to lecture, a teaching situation: "When Hegel is explained, it is always in a seminar and in telling students: the history of the concept, the concept of history," Derrida writes in a left-column judas pocket. The concept of history is familial; it raises the father in the son, returns the self to itself: "Rearing (the student), *l'élève*. What is *élever* in general (*élevage*, *élévation*, *élèvement*, breeding, elevation, education, upbringing)? Against what is rearing (*une élève*) practiced?" (G 15ai). Against the merely natural, the embodied, education dissolves the family, raises only in crossing the woman out; enables the father, through the rearing of the son, to hold on to himself. Pulling on the family thread, Derrida works over this logic of the *Aufhebung*, "the essential—and not only figurative—affinity between the movement of relief (*relève, Aufhebung*) and rearing (the student) (*l'élève*) in general: *élévation, élèvement, élevage*, elevation, breeding, education, upbringing. Airy ascent of the concept. *Begriff* grasps and sweeps upward, opposes its force to everything that falls (to the tomb)" (G 23ai). To resist this upward sweep of the concept, the passage to *Sa* that cuts off both ear and tongue, Derrida foregrounds, in radical ways, the materiality and supplementarity of language; he grafts words onto each other, slices them open to release multiple signifieds that cannot be gathered, and throws his own name into a game of "agrammatical non-sense" (Ulmer 1986, 35b). This is about "hearing otherwise," Ulmer contends: "Derrida, in short, goes after the ear" (35c), not the ear of *Sa*, but the ear of *glas*:

> (the) *glas* rings [*tinte*] near (the) *tétine* [teat]. (The) *tétine* [teat] resounds and reverberates [*retentit*]. The possibility of adding the article between parentheses assumes this interval and this passage (rhythm of sucking [*ventouse*]) between uses (between, if one still wants, the use as signifier, the use as signified, the use as referent). It has to do with yielding to the necessity that associates, in the maximum of use and of over-use, the greatest number of marks, as for example *la tétine qui retentit dans un glas* [the teat that reverberates in a *glas*]. Who has ever heard that (*ça*)? That tintinnabulum there? (G 153bi, cited in Ulmer 1986, 35c–37b)

David Farrell Krell points out that "*savoir absolu* can be heard in French as *s'avoir absolu*, absolute self-having or self-possession, so that the goal of absolute knowing and the fantasy of perfect presence to self appear to be indistinguishable" (Krell 2000, 151). Such is the case in Hegel, where self-presence is an absolute holding on to speech, binding it to, *hearing it within*, oneself, *banding erect*. Pulling on the thread of the family, however, causes the institutional edifice to slacken: the countersignature here as *contra-band*. This counter-signing would be women's work: in pulling on the family thread, Derrida falls in with the delirious women—in the East—whom Hegel describes in his *Aesthetics* (II, 641), women who participated in Dionysiac fertility rituals by pulling on the thread of a huge phallus, "a crowd of frenzied females (*als ein Haufen schwärmender Weiber*), the unleashed (*ungebändigte*) delirium of nature" (G 234a). While in Hegel's family history, both the woman and the East figure a middle that gets gulped down; in *Glas*, the middle, the figure, remains and cannot be consumed.[13] "Remains entail a loss of integrity," Krell observes (Krell 2000, 153). Covered with tattoos, wounded and scarred, the *Glas* columns spill undigested material into the middle space; the closed circle opens to the leftovers of Hegel's Last Supper meal; to the mortal remains of the woman he would have disappear; to the bodies of all the others that the logic of the *Aufhebung* has helped to inter or incinerate. "What remains," Krell writes, "is precisely what passes, decomposes, and in the stench of its corruption—the green spots of decay on its exquisite hands—elaborates the very definition of what is *inessential* for philosophy" (153). This is the key: it is through (as) what is *inessential*, yet *indigestible* ("And what if what cannot be assimilated, the absolute indigestible, played a fundamental role in the system, an abyssal role rather, the abyss playing an almost trans-" [G 151a]) that Derrida countersigns *Sa*, making *Glas* a legend of remnants or remains, "crypting the signature so that it becomes impossible to spell it out" (Spivak 1977, 24), and so that the signifier cannot give way to a signified. "The debris of d-words is scattered all over the pages" (24).

GLAS SOUND

> If, on the other hand, a bell is cracked, we hear not only the vibration but also other forms of material resistance, the brittleness and irregularities of shape, then we have an impure sound, a noise.
>
> —Hegel, *Philosophy of Nature*

A legend could be a life story. *Glas* is, among other things, about this story's remainders. Not only a bastardized work, a monstrous composite/collage of life-and-work genres, an "ensemble of morsels that no longer proceed from the whole and that will never form altogether one" (G 227a), *Glas* is also a book full of bastards. Some of these—the mother of Genet, Antigone, sister of Polynices, and of course, Hegel's estranged sister, Christiane—are highly visible in the book; others—Hegel's illegitimate son Ludwig Fischer, for instance—are present as specters. In either case, the bastards of *Glas*, male and female alike, are what Hegel's family cannot relieve or assimilate; thus they are what keeps the circle of *Sa* from closing, "an element excluded from the system that assures the system's space of possibility?" (G 162a).[14] Derrida calls them "my bastards" (PT 51). In this legend of remains, their names are encrypted in his "polysexual signature" (107), in the "bastard path" it inscribes. What matters here is the signature's (signifier's) movement.

"A bastard course. Is there a place for the bastard in ontotheology or in the Hegelian family?" (G 6a), Derrida asks early in the left column. As a Jew, Derrida is a bastard, an "absolute indigestible" himself; for, according to Hegel, there can be no father-son filiation in Judaism, no family, no nation. Like the deaf and mute woman, the Jew belongs to darkness and death. "The Jew is dead, castrated," Derrida writes; the Jew "materializes everything he touches" (G 44a). The Jew, Hegel says, is a Medusa who turns everything to stone: "Like the Gorgon, the Jew materializes, petrifies everything he sees and everything that regards him" (G 45a).

Derrida, the polysexual-bastard-Jew, materializes sound, so that in *Glas*, and as the *glas* of *Sa*, "words make noise and strike the ear" (G 93bi). So that the tongue remains, in the throat, as in *cataglottism*, from a right column judas pocket (use of abstruse words; also tongue, language [see Gloss, *glose*]): "The ACLs sound, clack, explode " (G 2bi). So that the tympan between the two columns takes on the look of an "old parchment crossed every which way, overloaded with hieroglyphs" (PT 106): *catachresis*, from the same right column, another judas tattoo, is the movement of this crossing (as in "a word diverted from its proper sense;" also, a musical term: "Harsh and unfamiliar dissonance" [G 2bi]). The countersignature, the "zigzagging, oblique to boot" (G 5a) *passage* of Derrida's d-stroke, crossing back-and-forth between the columns—"tolling the *glas*, oscillating dissymmetrically from one column to another with a vertiginous movement in between" (Spivak 1977, 26)—*spaces*.[15]

No eating of voice or ear. If *Glas* is a work of mourning (*catafalque*, again from the right column, same set of judases: "platform raised as an honor, in the middle of a church, to receive the coffin or effigy of a deceased " [G 2bi]), it has to do with (what) remains.

FOUR

WHO HAS EARS TO HEAR?

Where is an ear? What is the inside and the outside of an ear? What is
it, for an ear, to (be) open? What is it to prick up one's ear [*tendre
l'oreille*]? To hear [*entendre*] or not to hear? To be deaf, not to be able or
to be unwilling to hear, perhaps in the sense in which Heidegger will
speak later (1933–34), about Hölderlin's *Der Rhein*, about mortals that
turn, as is said in French and English, a "deaf ear: (*das Überhören*)? "
. . . . Where then is the ear that we lend, as is said in French and
English, in particular the ear we lend to the voice of the friend?
What is the ear, in the literal [*propre*] sense, if there is such a
sense? What, properly speaking, is the ear, the ear as such and in
its singularity?

— Derrida, "Heidegger's Ear: Philopolemology (*Geschlecht* IV)"

TIME 1: SILENCE

"NOT A WORD FROM HEIDEGGER," Derrida observes (G1 66). In
Being and Time, Heidegger maintains an "impressive silence" (66) on
the question of sexual difference. Offering his existential analytic of
Dasein not as an inquiry into this or that positive science, but as a
foundational, fundamental, ontology from which alone all university
disciplines derive, Heidegger yet holds to a "manifest silence" (66) on
sexual difference. It is as if *Dasein* would have no sex, as if, in Derrida's
words, "sexual difference did not rise to the height of ontological
difference" (66). Following Kant and Hegel in this tradition of philosophy of university, how could Heidegger not concern himself with
height, "what height is in the question, the thought of difference not

63

rising to any" (66)? How could he not concern himself with sexual difference when, among "the best educated and endowed 'modernity'" (66–67), some discourse on sexuality is deemed necessary to university footings? What might we make of Heidegger's silence on sex in *Being and Time*? And given that his silence elsewhere has so preoccupied Heidegger's critics, what might we make of their silence on his remaining silent here? Derrida's first study of Heidegger to appear under the name *Geschlecht* opens on "this scene of a stubborn mutism at the very center of the conversation, in the uninterrupted and distracted buzzing of the colloquium" (66) on philosophical—and institutional—foundations. "Who, indeed, around or even long before him has not chatted about sexuality as such, as it were, and by that name? All the philosophers in the tradition have done so, from Plato to Nietzsche, who for their part were irrepressible on the subject. Kant, Hegel, Husserl have all reserved it a place; they have tried at least a word on it in their anthropology or in their philosophy of nature, and really everywhere" (66).

Thus far, *Geschlecht*, "that frighteningly polysemic and practically untranslatable word" (OS 7), appears in the title of four of Derrida's readings of the work of Martin Heidegger, as well as being central to his discussion in *Of Spirit: Heidegger and the Question*, the volume that, as David Farrell Krell puts it, "interrupts the genetic transmission from the (unpublished) third to the (recently published) fourth generation" *Geschlecht* (Krell 1992a, 252). While "no word, no word for word will suffice to translate this word that gathers in its idiomatic value stock, race, family, species, genus/gender, generation, sex" (GII 183)—not the least, sex—*Geschlecht*, with all its multiple meanings, inevitably touches on the matter of life. Derrida's *Geschlecht* publications thus contribute to the "history of life" that he begins to imagine in *Of Grammatology*, history of life articulated as a history of the *grammè* (OG 84). Such "history" would be "larger" than man ("one could speak of a 'liberation of memory,' of an exteriorization always already begun" [84]), not receiving its guiding concepts from the *human* sciences or from traditional metaphysics and, like Heidegger's existential analytic, grammatology would be foundational, not "just one *regional science* among others" (83). If Derrida's first *Geschlecht* constitutes a point of departure for this grammatological discourse of foundations, it does so by listening to Heidegger's silence on sex in *Being and Time*, the work that Heidegger put forward as itself a new point of departure.

Heidegger's silence on sex belongs to a time—the year is 1927—and to a modality of writing that also maintains a silence on "spirit" and the "spiritual," on the words *Geist* and *geistlich*: in *Being and Time*, Derrida points out, these are words that Heidegger takes care to avoid. Critics make no mention of this caution around spirit; indeed, "[n]o one ever speaks of spirit in Heidegger," Derrida claims in *Of Spirit* (3–4). "Not only this: even the anti-Heideggerian specialists take no interest in this thematics of spirit, not even to denounce it. Why? What is going on? What is being avoided by this?" (4).[1] Why is Heidegger's early silence on spirit not treated as significant when, only a few years after *Being and Time*, in 1933, in a context that is highly charged politically and closely tied to the meaning he gives at that moment to *Geschlecht*—to history, language, nation, and national university—spirit is drawn upon, affirmed, even exalted? How does Heidegger's avoidance of spirit in 1927 relate to his invocation of it in 1933—in a discourse on the university? Does his early attempt at avoidance fail? To ask these questions is, for Derrida, to raise the larger question of avoidance itself: "How to avoid saying or speaking?" (HAS 25). How to speak or write outside of, in excess of, the either/or oppositions of the university discourse we have examined thus far in this book? How to speak or write otherwise? If in *Being and Time*, by avoiding certain words—sex, spirit—Heidegger fails to free his new discourse of foundations from the subject/object, spirit/matter, man/woman binaries of a Kant or a Hegel, there is nonetheless, Derrida says, something to be learned from the 1927 attempt, something that—Heidegger is already learning this himself by 1935, Derrida suggests—is inscribed in the structure, the movement, of the *grammè*, the *trait*, or the mark. It is necessary, then, to ponder Heidegger's early silence on spirit and sex, and to follow the trajectory of these once-silenced words in his works before and after 1933. This is just the task Derrida undertakes in *Of Spirit* and in his four generations of *Geschlecht*. In this chapter, I will briefly outline the trajectory as Derrida charts it, a trajectory that passes through the mouth and the ear: it both establishes the limit, the end, of the modern-Kantian tradition of university, and, for Derrida at least, offers the possibility of the institution's renewal, of a university *living on*.[2]

We can begin with sex, with sexuality and sexual difference, the matter on which, in *Being and Time*, Heidegger has nothing to say. "Transitive and significant silence (he has silenced sex) which belongs, as he says, to a certain *Schweigen* ('*hier in der transitiven Bedeutung gesagt*'), to the path of a word [*parole*] he seems to interrupt. But what are the places of this interruption? Where is the silence working on that discourse? And what are the forms and determinable contours of that non-said?" (G1 67). By way of approaching these issues, Derrida goes in his first *Geschlecht* to what he calls "the margins" of *Being and Time*, to the lecture course on logic that Heidegger delivered in 1928 at the University of Marburg/Lahn (translated by Michael Heim as *The Metaphysical Foundations of Logic*). Here, only one year after *Being and Time*, Heidegger tries to speak, struggles to find ways to speak, to speak "without speaking," to speak *otherwise*, about the sexuality of *Dasein*. His attempt, in Section 10 of the lecture course ("The problem of transcendence and the problem of *Being and Time*"), involves consideration of the word, *Dasein*, which, as he has already specified in *Being and Time*, is chosen for its "neutrality," for the reason that, Heidegger says, the "being" at stake in his work on foundations—the being at, and as, the foundation—is not a self or a man. "How to avoid saying or speaking?" (HAS 25). How to write about what does not belong to humanism's anthropocentric scheme, to the binary difference of Western metaphysics, and to its privileging of a phonetic-phonocentric tongue? *Dasein*, Heidegger says, is not *either* a man *or* a woman; its "neutrality also indicates that *Dasein* is neither of the two sexes" (Heidegger 1984, 36). The word *Dasein* suggests not *Geschlecht*, a sex, either male or female, but *Geschlechtlosigkeit*, sexlessness or asexuality. This *Geschlechtlosigkeit* is not nothing, "is not the indifference of an empty void, the weak negativity of an indifferent ontic nothing" (136); not "the voidness of an abstraction, but precisely the potency of the *origin*, which bears in itself the intrinsic possibility of every concrete factual humanity" (137). "Neutral *Dasein* is never what exists" (137); rather, it is "the primal source" (137) that makes every existence possible. "The analysis of *Dasein* is thus prior to all prophesying and heralding world-views" (137).[3]

In "*Geschlecht*: sexual difference, ontological difference," Derrida works meticulously through this section of Heidegger's lecture course where the distinction between *Geschlecht* and *Geschlechtlosigkeit* is set out. What makes for something new in this point of departure is the *spacing* that, Derrida says, Heidegger's *Geschlechtlosigkeit* puts in place from the start. I have been arguing in this book that there can be no embodied hearing without spacing to an outside; and that spacing entails movement, vibrations, and an imprint of some sort. It is just such spacing movement that is suggested by *Geschlechtlosigkeit*. In the 1928 lecture course, Derrida notes, Heidegger distinguishes the point of departure for his discourse of foundations from the ideal self-proximity of a Kant or a Hegel and insists that being does not begin—or end—with a (male) self, close-to-itself and at home with itself: neutral *Dasein* is not "the egocentric individual, the ontic isolated individual" that, as we have seen, is "the center of the entire problematic" (Heidegger 1984, 137). Since *Dasein* is embodied from the start and primordially thrown into multiplicity, *spacing is originary*: neutral *Dasein* is characterized by "dissemination in space" (138). "*Dasein*'s relation to itself: it is dispersed," is the way that Derrida puts it. "*Erstreckung* names a spacing which, 'before' the determination of space as *extensio*, comes to extend or stretch out being-there, the there of Being between birth and death" (G1 77). On this *Erstreckung*, the *Streuung* and the *Zer-streuung*, Heidegger's lecture course is, Derrida points out, "fraught with translation problems" (75) that any attempt to summarize quickly can only aggravate. This point, however, can be made: "An 'originary dissemination (*ursprüngliche Streuung*)' belongs already to the Being of *Dasein*" (76). Heidegger's analytic is not "founded" on traditional (Kantian, Hegelian) notions of pure consciousness or spirit or spiritual interiority, according to which, as Derrida puts it in *Of Spirit*, "a man, a spiritual thing, would see himself *after the fact* (*nachträglich*) transposed, transferred, deported (*versetzt*) into a space" (OS 24). Heidegger wants to avoid this binarity of a before and an after, as well as all of the oppositions that go along with it: presence/absence, spirit/matter, mind/body, self/other: dissemination—scattering, dispersion, spacing—is, in the 1928 lecture course, "a structure of originary possibility" (G1 76).

In proposing this condition of originary deferral, Heidegger also wants to avoid reducing neutral *Dasein* to either of the two sexes. The avoidance is not about desexualizing *Dasein*: "If *Dasein* as such belongs to neither of the two sexes, that doesn't mean that its being is deprived of sex. On the contrary, here one must think of a pre-differential, rather a pre-dual, sexuality—which doesn't necessarily mean unitary, homogeneous, or undifferentiated" (G1 72). *Dasein*'s neutrality "would be a matter of the positive and powerful source of every possible 'sexuality.' The *Geschlechtlosigkeit* would not be more negative than *aletheia*" (72). One must think, then, outside of either a one or a two, either unity or binarity; one must think of (a) being as already marked (an *imprint* already in place at the origin) and dispersed (*spacing-*

movement as the point of departure) in its own body: this being dissociated, separated (from self-proximity), as the originary structure affecting *Dasein*. Along the lines proposed in *Of Grammatology*, Derrida reads the beginning as *written*: at the origin is "the written Being/the Being written" (OG 18), rather than a signified concept, a pure voice that is heard without borrowing from outside of itself. With Heidegger's *Geschlechtlosigkeit*, there is "no linguistic sign without writing" (14), and thus, no "effacement of the signifier in the voice" (20). This is a very different point of departure from the Kantian-Hegelian *hearing-oneself-speak*. The difference might allow for an embodied ear, for a university that can, in diverse ways, hear.

To suggest that neutral *Dasein* begins already written, although imprinted otherwise than with a binary sexual mark, is to introduce a "typological motif" that, for Derrida, has everything to do with the word-path he charts in Heidegger's texts before and after 1933. The *typos* is always at stake in Derrida's reading of "the political" in Heidegger, and by the same token, it is fundamental to his reading of "the university" in Heidegger's texts. The notion of a nonbinary mark that imprints *Dasein* from the start is one instance of this *typographé*: it suggests that, in what Derrida calls Heidegger's silence on sex in *Being and Time* (and its margins), we might find the possibility for a university discourse not founded on the transcendental voice, on the phonetic oral-aural privilege. The typographical motif as nonbinary mark is also at issue, for Derrida, in another 1927 scene of silence or avoidance, this one having to do with the word spirit, with Heidegger's silence on the word in *Being and Time*, and the critical silence on his silence. Not only is spirit marginal, parenthetical, "not a great word of Heidegger's" (OS 3) in *Being and Time*, it is, like sex, something he tries to avoid. On first mention, then, Heidegger specifies spirit as "the word no longer to use" (29). On second mention, however, when he must resort to the word, it is written "negatively, indirectly, silently" (24–25), inside quotation marks. Derrida refers to these quotation marks as "mute signs" (25): they cannot be made into phonemes or acoustic phenomena—he emphasizes this point; they are written signifiers, and they have to be seen, or signed, to be heard. No more than in the 1928 lecture course should these "negative," marks be understood as designating negativity, Derrida insists. But what is manifested by this silence on spirit in Heidegger, "[t]he silent play of the quotation marks" (66) that is evident not only in 1927 but also, with a difference that we will return to later in the chapter, in later texts? By his own account in *Being and Time*, Heidegger wants to avoid the spirit/matter, signified/signifier binary on which all of metaphysics is based. He wants to introduce his existential analytic as another point of departure. With the quotation marks around spirit, he would remind us of this: his point of departure is different; his spirit is not the spirit of metaphysics; his discourse, or the source for it, belongs to another, more originary and non-vulgar time.

What Heidegger wants to avoid, however, "will not be avoided all at once" (OS 56). The point is crucial to Derrida's assessment of the "failure" of Heidegger's attempted silence of 1927–28. In *Being and Time*, Heidegger would remove his discourse of foundations absolutely from contamination by the binarity of metaphysics. His "spirit" would be altogether different from the ideality of a Descartes or a Kant or a Hegel. His "spirit" would not be haunted by its double—and this is precisely the problem. "*Geist* is always haunted by its *Geist*," Derrida maintains. "Metaphysics always returns, I mean in the sense of a *revenant* [ghost], and *Geist* is the most fatal figure of this *revenance* [returning, haunting]. Of the double which can never be separated from the single" (40). If it is this double that Heidegger attempts to avoid in 1927, then Derrida must ask: "Is this not what Heidegger will never finally be able to avoid (*vermeiden*), the unavoidable itself—spirit's double, *Geist* as the *Geist* of *Geist*, spirit as spirit of the spirit which always comes with its double?" (40–41).

I read Derrida to say, in *Specters of Marx*, that once a discourse declares itself free of haunting, once the new order is announced as arrived, all movement of deferral stops, and we are squarely back into metaphysics and all of its binaries. The cessation of movement in Heidegger takes less than six years.

TIME 2: BENUMBEDNESS

Of course our hearing organs are in a certain regard necessary, but
they are never the sufficient condition for our hearing, for that
hearing which accords and affords us whatever there really is to hear.

—Heidegger, *The Principle of Reason*

Indeed, the difficulty is already evident in 1928 in the discourse on the animal that Heidegger initiates in *The Fundamental Concepts of Metaphysics*. In 1928, but also in later texts such as *What Is Called*

Thinking? (*Was heisst Denken?* 1951–52), Heidegger's writing on animality inevitably reinstates the metaphysical either/or that in *Being and Time* he set out to avoid. For on the matter of what differentiates the animal from the human *Dasein*, Derrida remarks in his second *Geschlecht*, Heidegger "inscribes not some differences but an absolute oppositional limit" (GII 174). This is certainly the case in *The Fundamental Concepts of Metaphysics* where, only one year after the Marburg lecture course, with the single stroke of a silencing-deletion, space and spacing disappear into before/after linear time and the man/animal hierarchy. Not incidentally, it is by way of this anthropocentric hierarchy that Heidegger moves, between 1929 and 1935, into an affirmation of spirit as what distinguishes the human *Geschlecht* from the animal. And where the man/animal binary is put in place, other related (sexual, racial, national, and linguistic) hierarchies are also reinscribed, as happens in the Rectorate Address. Thus, to use Derrida's words, Heidegger's discourse on the animal has a "political destination" (173). The university, the hierarchy of university disciplines, is always at issue in this discourse. What is very significant about the discourse, for my purposes in this book and for contemporary criticism overall, is that Heidegger's affirmation and elevation of spirit, and the spiritual world of the human *Geschlecht*, "our *Geschlecht*" (173), takes place as his withdrawal from a speechless—deaf and mute—os.

That animal deprivation comes down to its being deaf and dumb is a point toward which *The Fundamental Concepts of Metaphysics* builds from its opening pages. For what Heidegger wants to discuss in these pages—the kind of activity that philosophy is, a kind of "hearkening" or hearing, a mode of being "attuned"—already implies his distinction between hearing and having animal ears. Just what it is to hearken is a matter to which Heidegger returns again and again over the years, his persistence on the question perhaps not surprising given that, as he puts it in *What Is Philosophy?*, "destruction" means simply "to open our ears" and to hear (Heidegger 1958a, 73). The potential for such attunement, such attentive *being-there* to things, belongs alone to man, Heidegger states flatly in *The Fundamental Concepts of Metaphysics*: "*We name the being of man being-there, Da-sein*" (Heidegger 1995, 63). Of course, the possibility for *being-away* also belongs to man: witness the sciences ("to judge philosophy according to the idea of science is the most fateful debasement of its innermost essence" [2]), which are absorbed in questions that have nothing to do with, and must not be confused with, what thinking or philosophizing is. Philosophy's hearkening, driving us out of our everydayness and "back into the ground of things" (21), is what makes for its institutional privilege ("Philosophy does not exist because there are sciences, but vice-versa: there can be sciences only because and only if there is philosophy" [22]), and is what effectively reconstitutes the Kantian hierarchy of the disciplines, even as Heidegger claims that philosophy is an activity ("Philosophy is philosophizing" [4]), not just a discipline like all the others.[4] It's the same hearkening that, in later texts, he associates with "the hand," the hand that "brings about the 'work' of destruction" (Heidegger 1992, 80), the work of opening ears to hear. The hand exists as hand only where there is hearkening, which is to say that the scientist or technician, in his mode of questioning, is not a "man of the hand." Yet, while man's hand can be withdrawn from its essence, his retention of the potential for the handwork of hearkening is what sets him apart from the animal: "No animal has a hand, and a hand never originates from a paw or a claw or talon" (80). This means that no animal has an ear, no "ear capable of hearing" (GIV 172). The conclusion is already reached in *The Fundamental Concepts of Metaphysics* where the man/animal binary is firmly constructed. For, Heidegger explains in *The Fundamental Concepts*, although man has the potential for being-away, even for lapsing, *temporarily*, into a dazed animal-like state, he is distinguished by a capacity for hearkening that the animal lacks. Herein lies the difference between "the *essence of the animality* of the animal and the *essence of the humanity* of man" (Heidegger 1995, 179).

What Heidegger calls his "comparative" method in this discourse is undertaken by means of three theses: the stone is worldless; the animal is poor in world; man is world-forming (Heidegger 1995, 185). It is in this elaboration of *world* that spirit wrests itself free of the quotation marks that, in 1927, were marks of a discourse of the other. And as much for Heidegger here as for Hegel, when spirit struggles free, it rises away from inanimate stone. The stone is what gives meaning to Heidegger's differentiation of *Dasein* from the animal, Derrida notes in *Of Spirit* ("It would be necessary, precisely around the problem of animality, to reelaborate the question of Heidegger's relationship to Hegel" [OS 50]), for the stone, unlike the animal, represents negativity, "pure and simple absence" (50). As Heidegger puts it, the stone has "no being at all" (Heidegger 1995, 179): it cannot even be called dead since it is never alive. In its "being away" the stone is "precisely *not* there" (64). No question of *deprivation*, then, where the stone is concerned; no question of loss, since the stone has nothing to lose. The case with the animal, however, is different, and this is Heidegger's point: the animal is alive and does relate to the world around it, although in an impoverished ("world-poor") way that falls short of *Dasein*'s hearkening attunement. Being impoverished here means "*being deprived [Entbehren]*" (195), "having a lack or insufficiency" (195) that permanently precludes the possibility of an attuned *being-there*. As Derrida summarizes Heidegger's argument on animal deprivation, and indeed, on the essence of what it is to be deprived:

> The animal can have a world because it has access to entities, but it is deprived of a world because it does not have access to entities *as such* and in their Being. The worker bee, says Heidegger, knows the flower, its color and its scent, but it does not know the flower's stamen *as* a stamen, it does not know the roots, the number of stamens, etc. The lizard, whose time on the rock, in the sun, Heidegger describes laboriously and at length (and it makes one long for Ponge), does not relate to the rock and the sun *as such*, as that with regard to which, precisely, one can put questions and give replies. And yet, however little we can identify with the lizard, we know that it has a relationship with the sun—and with the stone, which itself has none, neither with the sun nor with the lizard. (OS 51-52)

What seems to me all-important about Heidegger's discussion here, and about Derrida's reading of it, is the linking of deprivation to loss both of hearing—the animal lacks an ear for being—and of speech. The animal cannot open its ear and neither can it speak, "put questions and give answers," as Derrida states above. The word that translates this dual deprivation for Heidegger—the essence of the animal state as deaf and dumb—is benumbedness (*Benommenheit*). The word both draws from and supports the phonocentric notion that to be mute (i.e., "dumb," lacking speech) is to be dull; and as I argue in the opening pages of this book, one is "dumb" (i.e., dull, lacking mind or *animus*) in this tradition *because* one is deaf (Heidegger himself notes in *Der Satz vom Grund* that to be deaf is to be dull: his word in this instance is *tumb*, the Old High

German form of *dumm* [Heidegger 1991, 47]). David Farrell Krell points out that "*Benommen* is the past participle of *Benehmen* and means 'disturbed, dazed, dizzy, dazzled, confused, mildly anesthetized, stupefied, stunned.'" In popular usage, *Benommenheit* means "dull-witted, stupid" (Krell 1992a, 9). To explicate the meaning of the word, Heidegger turns to the *benommen* bee, which is a telling example to say the least, given that, as Derrida notes, bees have had such a long history in Western metaphysics since Aristotle, and this for the reason that they are deaf (also sexless, according to Schelling): "Bees know many things, since they can see; but they cannot learn, since they are among the animals that lack the faculty of hearing. Thus, despite appearances to the contrary, the university, the place where people know how to learn and learn how to know, can never be a kind of hive" (PR 4). With the *benommen* bee, says Heidegger, there is no hand, "no apprehending [*Vernehmen*], but only a behaving [*Benehmen*]" (Heidegger 1995, 247); the bee cannot reach out to something as something, because it is *captivated* ("captivation is the essence of animality" [248]) or *self-absorbed*, closed within a circle, a ring [*Ring*], that it cannot escape (249).

What Heidegger in his essentializing way describes as "the animal"—unable, in its stunned self-absorption, to reach out to the surrounding world—seems to me rather to describe the condition of the architect-philosopher I have been examining in this book: Kant's philosopher of pure reason, for instance, gathered close-to-himself within the university's interior, altogether withdrawn from the other-outside, his ears and tongue cut off. And isn't this what I have been calling the Medusa effect, whereby the philosopher himself becomes a figure of the aural-oral lack away from which he withdraws? In Kant and Hegel, the withdrawal into *spirit*, a disembodied oral and aural ideal, leaves the philosopher, and the philosophical institution, "within the vault of its autism" (MP xvi), unable to speak or hear. We find a similar gesture of withdrawal and silencing in Heidegger. The gesture involves a typological motif that differs radically from the "mute signs" and mode of avoidance of *Being and Time*, and that, with the force of a single blow ("in one stroke [*Du coup*]" [GIV 173]), strikes through and crosses out. This crossing-through (*Durchstreichung*), in erasing "the word" (Heidegger 1995, 198), designates the animal's lack of ear and tongue, its incapacity to hear or speak the *as such* of things. "The erasing would mark in *our* language, by avoiding a word, this inability of the animal to name" (OS 53).

In 1929 and *The Fundamental Concepts of Metaphysics*, the speechless animal is characterized as deprived, impoverished in world, and therefore, poor in spirit. By 1935 and *An Introduction to Metaphysics*, however, as if to leave no doubt about the abyss of difference that separates the *os mutum* from speaking *Dasein*, Heidegger declares first that "[w]orld is always the world of *spirit*," and then adds, in the very next sentence: "The animal has no world nor any environment (*Umwelt*)" (Heidegger 1959, 45). The "inevitable consequence" of this statement is, as Derrida remarks, that "the animal has no spirit since, as we have just read, every world is spiritual. Animality is not *of spirit*" (OS 47). The *Durchstreichung* now demarcates "an absolute limit between the living creature and the human *Dasein*" (54). And yet, according to Derrida, this total withdrawal of spirit from the animal in the *Einführung* of 1935 simply "repeats" (41) the rhetoric of Heidegger's 1933 Rectorate Address, where not only "with the force of single blow" (31)[5] is spirit fully released from its 1927 marks of deferral but also, in the context of the spectacle of an academic inauguration, it is celebrated as having arrived:

> Six years later, 1933, and here we have the Rectorship Address: the curtain-raising is also the spectacle of academic solemnity, the splendor of the staging celebrating the quotation marks' disappearance. In the wings, spirit was waiting for its moment. And here it makes its appearance. It presents itself. Spirit *itself*, spirit in its spirit and in its letter, *Geist* affirms itself through the self-affirmation of the German university. (31)

The celebration "corresponds properly, literally, to an *exaltation* of the spiritual," Derrida writes. "It is an elevation" (OS 37), to the highest remove ("such a height" [39]), of everything on which Heidegger confers spiritual legitimacy. "One could say that he spiritualizes National Socialism" (37) at the same time that he declares a "spiritual imprint" to have been delivered to the German people, an imprint [*Gepräge*] that is said to mark their destiny, "the being-German of the people and of their world" and especially of the German university, "its university as will to know and will to essence" (38). Here again, Derrida calls attention to the typological, or the "onto-typological" (34), motif that is involved in Heidegger's withdrawal and elevation of spirit: the imprint is aligned with a "spiritual force" (39) and always is what gathers, what is unified and unifying. In this strange instance of the Medusa effect, the imprint that, with the force of one blow, exalts and elevates spirit and the German university as the essence of being-German, is also, in the same stroke and with the same force of a single blow, an essentializing, unifying *Durchstreichung* that strikes the animal out. Once he so designates the animal's "otherness" (Heidegger 1995, 177), Heidegger ceases to maintain a discourse of the other; the spiritual stamp stops the movement of deferral. This is the "terrifying moment" (OS 31) when Heidegger himself is dumbstruck. Hereafter, he speaks not a single word about or against the event associated with the atrocities of Nazism.[6] He is deaf to all questions. He never responds.

That Heidegger withdraws spirit *away from the mute (animal) mouth* is a point made clear not only by the argument on animal deprivation of *The Fundamental Concepts of Metaphysics*, but also, perhaps even more so, by "the *spiritual* quality which defines the absolute privilege of the German language" (OS 68) for Heidegger after 1929. The privilege Heidegger accords to the German in his Rectorate Address, and in *An Introduction to Metaphysics* to the German along with the Greek, sets up a "dissymmetry," to use Derrida's word, between those two languages and all other languages (and all other peoples) of the world (69). One can *hearken*, it seems, only in a language that is "capable of naming, of calling up Being—or, rather, of hearing itself called by Being" (69): only in a language capable of *hearing-itself-speak*. It turns out that this language, for Heidegger, is German alone, "that of the two twinned languages, Greek and German, which have in common the greatest spiritual richness, only one of them can name what they have and are in common par excellence: spirit" (71). And since, as Derrida notes, "to name is to offer for thinking," German is, according to Heidegger, "the only language, at the end of the day, at the end of the race, to be able to name this maximal or superlative (*geistigste*) excellence which in short it shares, finally, *only up to a certain point* with Greek. In the last instance, it is the only language in which spirit comes to name itself" (71). Heidegger's privileging of this language has, again to use Derrida's words, "an irreducible bond to the question of humanity versus animality" (GII 165), for while the singularity of the German tongue creates a dissymmetry between "our *Geschlecht*" and all other races and languages, it even more pointedly targets the animal as this argument's absolute other: the animal, the being deprived altogether of speech, and thus, it goes without saying, altogether incapable of speaking German. And what about so-called "deaf and dumb" humans? What about those individuals who are born deaf and left permanently without speech—without a system of *phonetic language* such as German so superlatively is? Would Heidegger's privileging of "naming"—in German—also disinherit these, or at least create a dissymmetry between "our *Geschlecht*" and those who are, not temporarily dazed, but permanently disabled, deprived forever of hearing and speech? I will return briefly to these difficult questions in the concluding segment of this chapter.

By way of closing this discussion for now, let me add, however, that while Heidegger targets the animal, and for the reason that it cannot hear and cannot speak, the limit he demarcates between man and animal would also install a duality between the sexes, a duality that, I am arguing, traditionally and in the tradition of the modern university, has associated woman, as Medusa, with aural-oral loss. Heidegger cannot create a man/animal opposition without reinstating the man/woman binary. This is, as it were, "the price" of his "spiritualizing" strategy between 1929 and 1935. For "one cannot demarcate oneself from biologism, from naturalism, from racism in its genetic form, one cannot be opposed to them except by reinscribing spirit in an oppositional determination, by once again making it a unilaterality of subjectivity, even if in its voluntarist form" (OS 39).

TIME 3: THE EAR OF THE OTHER

For Derrida, *An Introduction to Metaphysics* is a pivotal text. For on the one hand, this is the text in which Heidegger declares the animal to be altogether without spirit, a declaration that would stop all differing/deferral; on the other hand, however, with the same text, Heidegger "renounces the project and the word ontology" and in his writing from 1935 onward, "nothing escapes the movement of the signifier" (OG 22). Even in *An Introduction to Metaphysics* itself, where the word *destitution* is discussed as "a movement proper to spirit" (OS 62), and where the word *Geistlichkeit* finds itself "doubled" (63), the transition to another time is underway. *The Question of Being (Zur Seinsfrage* 1956) belongs to this other time in that, Derrida says, when Heidegger crosses through the word Being in that text, when he proposes to put the word under erasure, the mark of deletion bears no resemblance to animal crossing-out; it does not represent "a negative sign or even a sign at all" (52). Rather:

> That deletion is the final writing of an epoch. Under its strokes the presence of a transcendental signified is effaced while still remaining legible. Is effaced while still remaining legible, is destroyed while making visible the very idea of the sign. In as much as it de-limits onto-theology, the metaphysics of presence and logocentrism, this last writing is also the first writing. (OG 23)

Given my argument in this book, that there can be no hearing without writing of some sort, this "first writing" might be a "first" move in the direction of a re-embodied hearing—and of a hearing university. Such is my reading of Derrida's reading of a "third ear" in Heidegger: something like the "third species" I discuss in chapter 6 (Plato's *chora* as a "*triton genus*"), this third ear does not belong either to phonetic interiority or to its opposite, the negativity of spiritual deprivation/ deafness. The third ear is given over to an unnameable other. What this ear attends to and receives is movement, vibrations, what shakes or oscillates, spaces, *between*. Vibrations are what produce the typological motif on which Derrida focuses in this instance, where the *typos* is not one or other kind of crossing/erasure, but the very movement, the back-and-forth movement, of crossing itself. *No hearing without an outside.*

The final pages of *Of Spirit* are given to a reading of this movement in *On the Way to Language* (*Unterwegs zur Sprache* 1953), which Derrida refers to as "one of Heidegger's richest texts: subtle, overdetermined, more untranslatable than ever" (OS 86). The path of certain words—*Geist, geistlich, geistig*—is again at issue in Derrida's reading, which opens by asking, "What is spirit?" (83) in the *Unterwegs*. In this text, twenty years after the Rectorate Address, Heidegger gives his "final reply" to that question, Derrida maintains. And now, "*Geist* is neither Christian *Geistlichkeit* nor Platonic-metaphysical *Geistigkeit*" (96). Indeed, when Heidegger writes in *On the Way to Language* that "spirit is flaming," is "flame" or what "inflames" (Heidegger 1971, 179; OS 84), his reply does not bring "the path of spirit" to a new meaning or concept, an ultimate signified, so much as it makes "a path of spirit," turns "spirit" into the oscillating, coming-going, path of the signifier, or better still, the *trait*. "Spirit *in-flames*, how is this to be *heard* or *understood* [*entendre*]? Not: what does it mean? But how does it sound and resound?" (OS 84).[7] Not what does it mean, but how does the coming-going movement produce sound: spirit here becomes a word for the way that language, rather than present-to-oneself, is inhabited by, and responds to, an other. Spirit, we might say, now evokes the *specter*, or the spectral (double) structure that language is, the coming-going of the specter that can be felt, and must be read, in every *trait*.

This is the sense of spirit that, for Derrida, would be marked in the back-and-forth between Heidegger and Trakl, thinker and poet: Heidegger's "*Gespräch* with Trakl, that collocution of *Denker* and *Dichter*, strikes the reply" (OS 83) to the question of spirit in 1953. For the Heidegger-Trakl *Gespräch*, rather than an acoustic-phonetic speech-and-hearing conversation, is given over to the movement of the language that speaks *between* both thinker and poet, the language that "speaks *between* them" and that "divides and gathers according to a law" (83). This, too, is the sense of "spiritual" (*geistlich*) as Heidegger reads it in Trakl: "Spiritual is the gait of the year, the revolutionary coming-going of the thing which goes (*geht*)" (89). Although Derrida says in *Of Spirit* that he has yet to analyze what *On The Way to Language* "says of *Geschlecht*, of the word *Geschlecht*, and also of the place (*Ort*), and of animality" (87), the path of these words would also change as a result of this transformation in the path of spirit, this becoming-path of spirit. In place of oppositional difference, Heidegger now introduces a structure of supplementarity, a supplementarity that, he proposes, is there before the beginning, a "supplement of originarity" (90). The proposition implies a new thinking of time, where presence/absence and before/after no longer determine the order of things, and where *dissymmetry* (recalling the dissemination intrinsic to *Geschlechtlosigkeit*, as Derrida reads this in his first *Geschlecht*), rather than identity, is the place from which to begin. Spirit, spiritual, year (time): reading these words in *On the Way to Language*, Derrida says, Heidegger "intends to show that Trakl's *Gedicht* (his poetic work if not his poems) has not only crossed the limit of onto-theology: it allows us to think such a crossing [*franchissement*]" (86).

This movement of crossing is also what Derrida hears in Heidegger's discussion in *On the Way to Language* of the foreigner or stranger (*ein Fremdes*) in Trakl. This stranger is "the other" who comes and goes like a "*revenant*" (OS 91). The latter term, while "not a word of Heidegger's," is faithful to what, in his texts, "hears the coming and going" of the other, the stranger, as hope and as promise "as a coming back [*revenir*] from night to dawn, and finally as the returning [*revenir*] of a spirit" (91). The *revenant*, a specter, is never present as such—is without either a name or a face—and thus does not belong to an ocularcentric discourse of presence. And as Derrida puts it in *Specters of Marx*, because we cannot see the specter, because we cannot submit this other to visual identification, "we must fall back on its voice" (SM 7).[8] Insofar as the voice of the specter or stranger comes and goes briefly in *Being and Time*, that book itself "shakes or oscillates between two times" (GIV, 193): between, on the one hand, Heidegger's outright avoidance of spirit in the book, barely giving it shelter within quotation marks (OS 29); and, on the other hand, the brief gesture of hospitality he extends to the specter, the friend, in a marginal passage from Section 34, "as in hearing the voice of the friend whom every *Dasein* carries with it" (Heidegger 1962, 206). With this friend, Derrida says, it is really a matter of the voice, and of a voice that reaches us through "a third ear" (GII 196, n38). This is the voice, the voice of the friend, that Derrida discusses in his fourth *Geschlecht* ("Heidegger's Ear: Philopolemology [*Geschlecht* IV"]). I will conclude this discussion with a few remarks on the voice of the friend—and its movement of crossing.

Derrida is taken with the "furtive and enigmatic brevity of the passage" (GIV 166) from Section 34. Just as furtive, he suggests, is the friend evoked in the passage, only this once in *Being and Time*, for the friend comes and goes without ever coming into view or being made the object of a mastering gaze: "The friend does not appear [*paraît, apparaît*]" (165). Heidegger gives the friend no identity, no determined figure and no proper name, Derrida notes: "The friend has no face, no figure [*figure*]. No sex. No name. The friend is not a man, nor a woman; it is not I, nor a 'self,' not a 'subject,' not a person" (165). And not a Platonic-Christian spirit either. Given the non-present presence of its being-there, and the "tangible intangibility" (SM 7) of its body, the friend would be a *revenant*. In his reading in "*Geschlecht* IV," Derrida wants "to mark strongly the role of the ear" (GIV 180) in Heidegger's passage on the friend, the friend who addresses *Dasein* through the voice. The voice of the friend is not "the purely inner voice of the *ego* in Husserl's *Logical Investigations*" (175), the voice that one *hears-oneself-speak*. "Here there is no phenomenon of ideal self-presence in the inner voice. It is really a matter of the voice of the other" (175).

As I read Derrida reading Heidegger, this is a voice that haunts metaphysical philosophy, and the philosophical institution, with a notion of responsibility (of university autonomy) that does not put the subject first, as the injunction's author and addressee. In hearing the voice of the friend, responsibility or answerability shifts from the first person, self-present, self to an other, as if this other dictated a kind of law of potentiality-for-being (Heidegger 1962, 206; GIV 174). To open to the other is, first of all, to abandon the acoustic-phonetic privilege of *hearing-oneself-speak*, as Derrida reads Heidegger to do in his evocation of the voice of the friend. For as figureless (*sans figure*) as its face, the voice of the friend offers no signified, but only the movement of the signifier. The friend is silent, in this sense, "says nothing determined" (175), Derrida writes. "Heidegger lends it no remark" (175). This above all, for Derrida: "the voice of the friend is not reduced to the phoneme or to the acoustic phe-nomenon" (174).[9] Hearing this voice "does not consist in an acous-tic phenomenon of the physiopsychological order" (173), which means that hearing here is not opposed to deafness. The voice of the friend "comes under neither an acoustics, a phonetics, or a phonol-ogy, nor a theory of signification" (187). The voice of the friend has to do with a haunting movement, "there-and-back, the going-and-coming" (183) spacing of a call (*Ruf*). Listening to (the movement of) this call that "comes and goes; here, toward presence, there, toward absence" (167) makes of *being-there*, in Derrida's reading of Heidegger, a matter of being carried *bei-sich*, beside, alongside or outside one-self, "beyond the acoustic phenomenon [to] what is outside us" (178).

With this haunting movement, the body in the crypt starts to stir, the university tympan begins at last to vibrate. If then, as Heidegger suggests, destruction/deconstruction means "to open our ears" (Heidegger 1958a, 73), it does so, at this time and through this third ear, as a work of *solicitation*, "(from the Latin) *soliciting*. In other words, *shaking* in a way related to the whole (from *sollus*, in archaic Latin 'the whole,' and from *citare*, 'to put in motion')" (WD 6).

GESCHLECHT GLOSS

The hand, *die Hand*, Heidegger says in *What Is Called Thinking?*, "is a peculiar thing" (Heidegger 1968, 16). The hand gestures and catches, pushes and pulls, reaches and extends, receives and welcomes, holds and carries—as if it were a body part distal to the forearm, the carpus, metacarpus, and fingers together. But not so, says Heidegger, who is lecturing here at Freiburg for the first time since he was banned from teaching after the war, and who, at this significant, we might even say inaugural, moment, is teaching what it is to teach, to teach thinking, in a university especially. In the research institution that the university has become, the danger is great, he says, that we will confuse thinking with science, whereas thinking is a work of the hand. And what Heidegger wants his students to know of the hand and of *Hand-Werk*, they will not find in a dictionary of medical science:

> In the common view, the hand is part of our bodily organism. But the hand's essence can never be determined, or explained, by its being an organ which can grasp. Apes, too, have organs that can grasp, but they do not have the hand. The hand is infinitely different from all grasping organs—paws, claws, or fangs—different by an abyss of essence. Only a being who can speak, that is, think, can have the hand and can be handy in achieving works of handicraft. (16)[10]

Establishing the "essential co-belonging" (GII 179) of the hand and speech, elevating man—who has an ear for being and thus who speaks to the essence of things—over the mute animal, and positing a hierarchy of the disciplines—those that deal in *Hand-Werk* over those that deal in technics—this passage, along with others like it, gathers Heidegger's foundational thinking back into the binary logic of metaphysics. And Heidegger's discourse on the hand—the single hand, and the hand in its singularity—is a discourse of *gathering*, not of dispersing, dissemination and deferral, but of gathering close to essence, gathering to the essence of the human *Geschlecht* and to the essential difference between "the human *Geschlecht*, our *Geschlecht*, and the animal *Geschlecht* " (173). Although chronologically, *What Is Called Thinking?* (1951–52) puts us post the shift to a new foundation that, Derrida suggests, begins to take shape in 1935 with *An Introduction to Metaphysics*, this passage on the hand and on animal lack returns us to a time of benumbedness—to Heidegger's persistent striking-through of the other whenever he is discussing the disabled (animal) *os*, and, as inseparable from this, his own unbroken silence. No matter what the date of the Heideggerian text, gathering, as Derrida says, "[g]athering together (*Versammlung*) is always what Heidegger privileges" (GII 182) in his essentializing discourse on the animal. The animal that is impoverished in world. The animal that has no hand, that has no friend, and that has no ear either. The animal that cannot hearken and so cannot speak (GIV 172).

Derrida captures something of this ambiguity, "the ambiguity of the Heideggerian situation with respect to the metaphysics of presence and logocentrism," when he says in *Of Grammatology* that Heidegger's work both transgresses metaphysics and is contained within it. But it is impossible to separate the two" (OG 22). Perhaps Derrida makes the same point when he says in his second *Geschlecht* that Heidegger's work is never "homogenous and is written with two hands, at least" (GII 189): along with the hand that gestures to the voice of the friend is the hand that gathers to essence. As well as two hands, then, there would be at least two ears. And if this is the case, the ear of the other would always have as its counterpart the ear of interiority, the ear that privileges phonetic speech and thus that withdraws from, crosses out, the "deaf-and-dumb." This is a conclusion that I resist. For if we do conclude on this point, that "it is impossible to separate the two"—the gesturing from the striking hand, the ear of the other from *hearing-oneself-speak*—then deafness, prelingual deafness at least, must needs remain philosophy's instrument of petrification; as lack, its limit case.

This is the note of resistance on which I will leave both Heidegger and Derrida here. It seems to me that in Heidegger's reinterpretation of destruction as hearing, pre-lingual deafness does represent a limit case. "We hear, not the ear," Heidegger says in *Der Satz vom Grund*. "Of course we hear through the ear, but not with the ear if 'with' here means the ear is a sense organ that conveys to us what is heard." And then, in the very next sentence, Heidegger makes his well-known allusion to Beethoven: "*If at some later time* the human ear becomes dull, that is, deaf, then it can be, as is clear in the case of Beethoven, that a person nevertheless still hears, perhaps hears even more and something greater than before" (Heidegger 1991, 47, emphasis mine). Beethoven, of course, could speak, having become deaf "at some later time." But what does this passage say about the capacity for attunement of the pre-lingually deaf? Can there be a deaf-and-mute *Dasein*? Is there hearkening in the play of signing hands? Hearing is about following, Heidegger says in *An Introduction to Metaphysics*; it "has nothing to do with the lobes of our ears." And yet, in the same passage, deafness serves as Heidegger's example of a limit case: For those who do not follow, he goes on to say, "[t]hose who merely hear by listening around and assembling rumors are and remain the *axynetoi*, the uncomprehending. They are described in [Heraclitus's] Fragment 34: 'Those who do not bring together the permanent togetherness hear but resemble the deaf'" (Heidegger 1959, 129–30).

Heidegger's ear, to use Derrida's words, "divides itself" in such passages as these; "it is divided in two" (GIV, 184). Derrida's ear, by his own argument, does the same. Thus, despite his challenging of the acoustic-phonetic privilege in Heidegger, especially in Heidegger's politically charged discourse on the animal, Derrida still concedes something to Heidegger on the matter of deafness as lack's extreme. Writing in his fourth *Geschlecht*, for instance, and with reference to Heidegger's "third ear," Derrida says that "[o]ne *could even be physically deaf*" without ceasing to carry the voice of the friend (163–64, emphasis mine). It is a passing reference, but it's not a minor point. The *glas*, the tolling bell of chapter 3, is muted (becomes a dumbbell) where no question is brought to philosophy's "othering" of the deaf-and-mute *os*.

FIVE

FOUR WAYS OF READING TWO PAIRS:

OF SHOES

> But the most effective deconstruction, and I have said this often, is
> one that deals with the nondiscursive, or with discursive institutions
> that don't have the form of a written discourse. Deconstructing an
> institution obviously involves discourse, but it also concerns some-
> thing quite other than what are called texts, books, someone's signed
> discourse, someone's teachings.
>
> —Derrida, "The Spatial Arts"

DERRIDA'S *THE TRUTH IN PAINTING*, with its four essays, "[f]our
times, then, *around* painting" (TP 11), inscribes itself on (as) a frame.
The question of framing occupies Derrida throughout the book, "the
frame philosophy imposes when it contemplates art" (Gilmour 1988,
519). Borrowing the title of his book from the correspondence of Paul
Cézanne who in 1905 wrote to Emile Bernard, "I owe you the truth
in painting and I will tell it to you" (TP 2), Derrida asks whether
meaning is, simply, internal to the frame, already there *in* painting, or
whether interpretation of "the truth in painting" involves some crossing of the line, of the below and above, of the outside and in.
Significantly for my purposes in this chapter, Derrida's "objection to
Heidegger" (SA 25) often turns on this very issue, for Heidegger's
tendency to locate truth *in* painting or in visual art—or poetry, poetic
speech—leads to the hierarchization (of the disciplines) I discussed in
chapter 4. In the present chapter, I consider Derrida's "objection" to
both Heidegger and Meyer Schapiro, two university professors, "two

Figure 2. *Self-Portrait with Bandaged Ear,* oil on canvas, by Vincent van Gogh, Arles 1889. Courtauld Institute of Art, London.

illustrious Western professors" (TP 260), who, in a "debate" with each other over ownership of van Gogh's painted shoes, repeat the "classical philosophical gesture" (SA 25) of locating truth in art. Reading this debate in the fourth essay of *The Truth in Painting*, "Restitutions of the truth in pointing [*pointure*],"[1] Derrida plays on the motif of correspondence, not just the exchange of letters between Heidegger and Schapiro, but their sharing, through a difference of opinion, of the same "discourse on truth" (TP 267). In their common concern to locate the truth in painting, Schapiro and Heidegger, for all their differences with each other, form something like a pair—one of the two pairs I discuss in this chapter.

Because I want to relate this debate about truth to the theorizing of postmodernism and the postmodern university, my chapter begins with the discussion of another interpretive pair: the van Gogh–Heidegger couple that Fredric Jameson introduces in his now-classic account of postmodernism as a cultural dominant. Jameson's "Postmodernism or, the Cultural Logic of Late Capitalism," published first as a 1984 essay in the *New Left Review* and then again as the lead chapter in a 1991 book by the same title, makes the case for an agreement between van Gogh and Heidegger over the meaning, and ownership, of van Gogh's painted shoes. Jameson presents this "van Gogh–Heidegger" interpretation as definitive of a high-modernist *depth hermeneutics* and, significantly, as identical with his own historical-materialist reading of art. Although he shares their discourse of truth, Jameson claims a different owner for the (paired) van Gogh shoes than does either Heidegger or Schapiro. And attaching the shoes to their proper owner is all-important in Jameson's case, for it is precisely the uncoupling and unpairing of painted shoes—their detachment from a truth-saying subject—that he deplores in "postmodern" art, particularly in the postmodern shoes of Andy Warhol. As if detached shoes were severed ears, Jameson recoils from Warhol's postmodern slippers because, he claims, they are deaf to history and have a mute mouth. I take up this point in what follows, where I read Jameson's "postmodernism" as another version of the Medusan fantasy of the disabled *os*; in his reading of the van Gogh–Heidegger pair, the fantasy is provoked by deaf and mute shoes. If postmodernism is a loss of the voice, however, high modernist shoes both hear and speak truth: this, I argue below, is the case for Jameson—and for Schapiro and Heidegger as well.

Considering the difference of opinion between Schapiro and Heidegger as to who owns van Gogh's painted shoes, entering my chapter as a fourth party to this debate, Derrida does not line up on one side or another so as to give us an additional pair. For Derrida, the issue is pairing itself, the correspondence in truth that both Schapiro

and Heidegger display; the way in which each of these two professors—I add Jameson as a third—sees himself, or rather, *hears-himself-
speak*, in the high-modern painted shoes. But even as he critiques the
Schapiro-Heidegger correspondence, Derrida locates another kind of
correspondence in Heidegger's *The Origin of the Work of Art*, another
"interlaced correspondence" (F *correspondance* L *correspondere* f. *cor-* =
com- together, one with another + *respondere* to answer; "The etymol-
ogy implies that the word was formed to express mutual response"
[OED]) that links responsibility to a crossing-effect. This crossing (of
the frame, of the above and below, of the inside and out) suggests the
back-and-forth, coming-going movement I discussed in the last chapter. The movement spaces, and therefore allows sound—and shoes—
to escape interiority and travel out into the world.

THE VAN GOGH–HEIDEGGER PAIR

> For a pair functions/walks [*marche*] with symmetrical, harmonious,
> complementary, dialectical oppositions, with a regulated play of
> identities and differences.
>
> —Derrida, *The Truth in Painting*

Central to Fredric Jameson's account of the modern to postmodern
transition is his reading of a van Gogh painting, "van Gogh's well-
known painting of the peasant shoes" (Jameson 1991, 6), as a canonical work of high-modernist visual art. The painting is paradigmatically
"modern," for Jameson, in that it reconstructs an initial historical
situation, in this case "the whole object world of agricultural misery,
of stark rural poverty, and the whole rudimentary human world of
backbreaking peasant toil, a world reduced to its most brutal and
menaced, primitive and marginalized state" and then, through "the
most glorious materialization of pure color" (7), reworks and transforms that situation altogether. This transformation "is to be seen as
a Utopian gesture," he writes, "an act of compensation which ends up
producing a whole new Utopian realm of the senses, or at least of that
supreme sense—sight, the visual, the eye" (7). Van Gogh's utopianism,
in turn, would be constitutive of the so-called "autonomy" of high
modern art: its dialectical capacity to replicate the specializations and
divisions of capitalist life, and yet at the same time, to find, in and
through such fragmentation, a revolutionary praxis.

Figure 3. *Draughtsman Drawing a Nude in Perspective*, woodcut, by Albrecht Dürer, 1527. The Metropolitan Museum of Art, New York.

Jameson's privileging of the visual is in keeping with the so-called ocularcentrism of modern culture, "the ubiquity of vision as the master sense of the modern era" (Jay 1988, 3). As is suggested by Albrecht Dürer's 1527 woodcut, *Draughtsman Drawing a Nude*, which is often cited by critics as an early model of this elevation of sight, modern specularity, its "gaze," goes along with a metaphysics of interiority or depth. The observer sees himself seeing through the painting to the meaning that it contains, as if the surface of the painting (page) were transparent, the open rectangle through which Dürer's draughtsman looks or the open window to which Alberti likened the painted canvas. For Jameson, this modern metaphysic of interiority, the "whole metaphysics of the inside and outside" (Jameson 1991, 11), entails what he calls an *aesthetic of expression* by virtue of which a painting, for all its silence, *speaks* the great modernist themes of alienation, anomie, isolation, and social fragmentation.[2] What distinguishes the modern, he says, is this "very aesthetic of expression itself" (11), which makes looking at an artwork a matter of listening to its internal truth. Seeing a painting is hearing what it says.

Jameson cites Heidegger's *The Origin of the Work of Art*, "a text which has always been very important to me" (Jameson 1982, 83), as a prime instance of this depth hermeneutics, especially those passages of *The Origin* where Heidegger reads van Gogh's painted shoes. For Heidegger, Jameson says, the van Gogh shoes not only re-create an initial situation, "the heavy tread of the peasant woman, the loneliness of the field path, the hut in the clearing, the worn and broken instruments of labor in the furrows and at the hearth," they allow for, even endorse, a utopian renewal: "Heidegger's account needs to be completed by insistence on the renewed materiality of the work, on the transformation of one form of materiality—the earth itself and its paths and physical objects—into that other materiality of oil paint affirmed and foregrounded in its own right and for its own visual pleasures" (Jameson 1991, 8). What Heidegger calls the rift between World and Earth is a dialectical tension between history and nature, Jameson says, between "the meaning-endowment of the historical project and the meaninglessness of organic life" (Jameson 1982, 83). Heidegger recognizes, Jameson claims, that the function of a great artwork, exercised through its visual power, is the staging of this dialectic. The function of the great artwork then, as Jameson reads *The Origin*, is the voicing of his own Marxist agenda: "the act of political revolution (the inauguration of a new society, the production or invention of radically new social relations)" (83). Jameson reads both van Gogh and Heidegger as speaking this (his) truth: in an act of critical ventriloquism, he drops his own voice into the "Van-Gogh-Heidegger shoes" (Jameson 1991, 10).

Figure 4. A *Pair of Shoes*, oil on canvas, by Vincent van Gogh, 1887. The Baltimore Museum of Art

What about these shoes, the painted shoes, however? What about "this painting," the "well-known painting of the peasant shoes," the "copiously reproduced image" (Jameson 1991, 6–7) to which Jameson says both he and Heidegger refer? Considering all the lectures he has given on the topic, you would expect the question to have come from someone in the class: which van Gogh painting is Professor Jameson (also supposedly Heidegger) reading here? For as Meyer Schapiro so emphatically reminds us, van Gogh painted a series of Still Life shoes, eight of which had been exhibited by the time Heidegger wrote *The Origin of the Work of Art*. Schapiro maintains that in *The Origin* Heidegger is discussing la Faille's no. 255, an 1886 canvas held in The National Vincent van Gogh Museum in Amsterdam. Neither in his 1984 essay nor in his 1991 book does Jameson take up this question of the painting, the question of which painting "this particular painting" (7) might be. Jameson's book does include an illustration; however, it is not of la Faille's no. 255 but of an 1887 canvas held in The Baltimore Museum of Art (Jameson titles it, "A Pair of Boots"). One might conclude then, that what he calls "the van Gogh–Heidegger shoes" do not form a pair after all, or at least that there is more than one van Gogh painting involved in Jameson's discussion and, if there is a pair, there are more than two shoes.

My suggestion is that for Jameson, the question of the painting is simply unimportant. For the use to which he puts it, any van Gogh shoe painting, indeed any high-modernist art work, will do just as well; the paintings are interchangeable because Jameson has them all *speak* the same truth. If we don't know which painting he refers to, if—despite that supreme utopian sense, "sight, the visual, the eye" (Jameson 1991, 7)—we don't know which painting to look at ("when we gaze at this particular painting" [7]), that does not matter to Jameson. What matters is that we *hear* what he (says the painting) has to say. Where the depth model of inside/outside is concerned, it is not the painted canvas itself but the truth spoken *in* painting that matters, and that truth, for Jameson, is the truth of the Hegelian dialectic, the truth of a dialectical history, alive and well and progressing, as it were, "on its left foot" (xi). Jameson *hears himself speak* in the painting(s). His interpretation makes van Gogh's Still Life shoes into a Jameson self-portrait. What matters is that the shoes come back to the dialectical subject from which, Jameson says, they set out. [3]

"Fetishism," in Freud's 1927 essay by that title, stems from a situation of looking, as Dürer's draughtsman is looking, at the body of a woman whose genitals are exposed to view. In Freud's essay, the woman in question is viewed from below, "from her legs up" (Freud 1927 [1961], 155), by an observing male, soon-to-be-a-subject, who might well be her son. What the inquisitive boy sees when his eyes move from the floor up the woman's skirt, is so traumatic, Freud says, that an immediate denial (*Verleugnung*) takes place.[4] "Probably no male human being is spared the fright of castration at the sight of a female genital," Freud writes (154). As a defense against this threat of detachment and as a denial of it, the boy fixes his eyes on the first object he sees—a shoe, possibly a woman's, his mother's, shoe—as substitute for the missing member. With this single substitute shoe, Freud says, castration "set[s] up a memorial to itself" (154).

According to Jameson, Andy Warhol's shoes are "clearly fetishes, in both the Freudian and Marxian senses" (Jameson 1991, 8). For one thing, the shoes are unpaired: from his first commercial enterprise in 1949, a full page of shoes, through the illustrations of Pomeroy's Shoe Poems and the many Miller shoe advertisements of the 1950s, Andy Warhol's shoes are "never in pairs" (Tyler 1956, 59). Jameson cites Derrida as remarking "somewhere" (which text?) that, for Heidegger, "the van Gogh footgear" (which painting?) are "a heterosexual pair," and thus allow "neither for perversion nor for fetishization" (Jameson 1991, 8). This is not Derrida's reading of Heidegger, I will argue in a moment. But it does suggest why Jameson is so anxious about Warhol's non-paired, non-heterosexual shoes. Freud (1927, 154–55) maintains that fur and velvet are often chosen as festishes because—like Medusa's serpent tresses—they register the *stigma indelebile* sight of the pubic hair. Might castration be the sight/fright that confronts Jameson in Warhol's postmodern shoes? For these shoes, in Jameson's own account, are problematically, perversely, single and severed from a heterosexual (dialectical) male subject. Moreover, the shoes are overlaid in gold leaf, painted with gold and silver trim, smothered in diamond dust, and decorated with strawberries, tassels, and feathers, fetishistic registers of the castration trauma. The high authenticity, the *being erect*, of van Gogh's shoes is missing for Jameson in the flaccidity ("hanging together on the canvas like so many turnips" [Jameson 1991, 8]), the lowness, of Warhol's shoes: in postmodernism, the autonomy of high art collapses, he says; the authentic art work "sink[s]

Figure 5. My *Shoe Is Your Shoe* (from the Portfolio: A *La Recherche du Shoe Perdu*), offset lithography, watercolor, and pen on paper, by Andy Warhol, 1955.

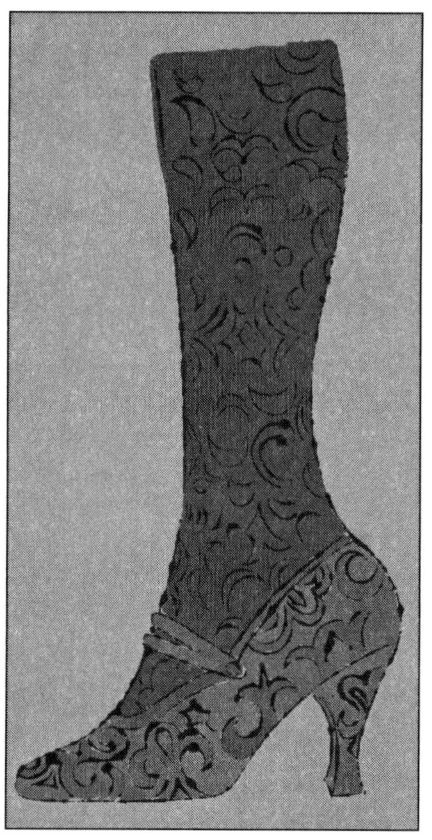

Figure 6. *Untitled (Shoe and Leg)*, ink and ink wash on paper, by Andy Warhol, c. 1956.

to the level of sheer decoration" (7). Superficial products of so-called mass or commodity culture, Warhol's shoes, like his Coca-Cola bottles and Campbell's soup cans, explicitly foreground the commodity fetishism of late capitalism, but in doing so, they offer no gesture of renewal. His shoes are impotent. For there is in Warhol "no way to complete the hermeneutic gesture" (8).

As I read it, Jameson's narrative of severance and loss suggests an aural-oral trauma. In the opening pages of *Postmodernism or, the Cultural Logic of Late Capitalism*, for instance, he describes postmodernism as, above all else, a state of deafness, "the matter of historical deafness" (Jameson 1991, xi). This is "an exasperating condition (provided you are aware of it) that determines a series of spasmodic and intermittent, but desperate, attempts at recuperation. Postmodern theory is one of those attempts: the effort to take the temperature of the age without instruments and in a situation in which we are not even sure there is so coherent a thing as an 'age,' or zeitgeist or 'system' or 'current situation' any longer" (xi). In an earlier work, Jameson describes "theory" as substitute-philosophy, a *prosthesis* fashioned out of ad hoc texts, "one would want to call it disposable theory" (Jameson 1988, 193), something that can be let fall on the floor next season when a newer fad comes along. Theory, especially that coming out of France, threatens philosophy "as a discipline and an institution" (193), he warns. The university, the institution of philosophy, is put at risk by postmodern textual practice, which goes so far as to *cut the sign off* from its referent, "from the signified, or from meaning proper" (200). To say that what is cut off here is an ear is not simply "to play"—as, Jameson says, theory does—with the trope of the ear in his work, and with the sexual investments that "powerfully constrain the *discourse of the ear*" (MP xiv) in his writing. For what is profoundly disturbing and alarming ("alarming new kinds of literary criticism based on some new aesthetic of textuality or *écriture*" [Jameson 1991, 1–2]) for Jameson about postmodern textual and artistic practices has to do precisely with their incapacity to hear and speak his truth.[5]

In Warhol's *Diamond Dust Shoes*, for example, the painted-printed shoes are detached, Jameson says, from a centered subject, an individual author, artist or ego (unless he is "deaf" to history, Jameson would have to acknowledge that this subject is male), and, as a result of this severance, the Warhol shoes are mute. "Andy Warhol's *Dia-*

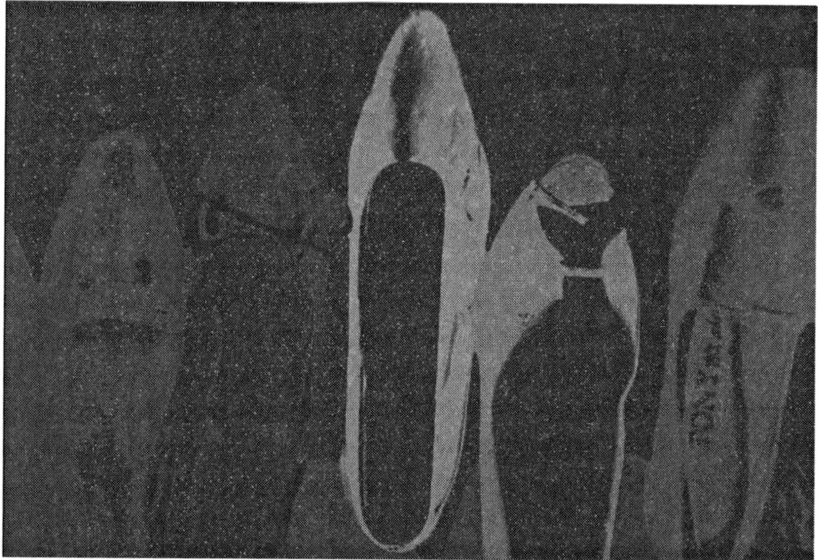

Figure 7. *Diamond Dust Shoes*, F&S 257, one from a portfolio of five screenprints with diamond dust printed on D'Arches Watercolor, by Andy Warhol, 1980.

mond Dust Shoes evidently no longer speaks to us with any of the immediacy of van Gogh's footgear; indeed I am tempted to say that it does not really speak to us at all" (Jameson 1991, 8). The *Diamond Dust Shoes* are speechless because they have nothing to say; no dialectical message, no immanent voice can be seen by Jameson in the depth of a postmodern painting. There is no way for him to step into Warhol's shoes. Not even the apparently paired ballet slippers on the January 1958 cover of *Dance Magazine* are assimilable to Jameson's dialectic, for where pointe shoes are concerned, unused and unworn ones at least, the left is indistinguishable from the right.[6] Jameson's is the kind of gaze I discuss in chapter 1: the gaze that separates the (heterosexual) male viewing subject from the feared object at which he looks, so that the subject is made transcendental and so that the viewed object—always othered and conflated with the body of the other sex—is reified and left for dead, like "the random collection of dead objects" (Jameson 1991, 8) Jameson sees in Warhol's *Diamond Dust Shoes*.

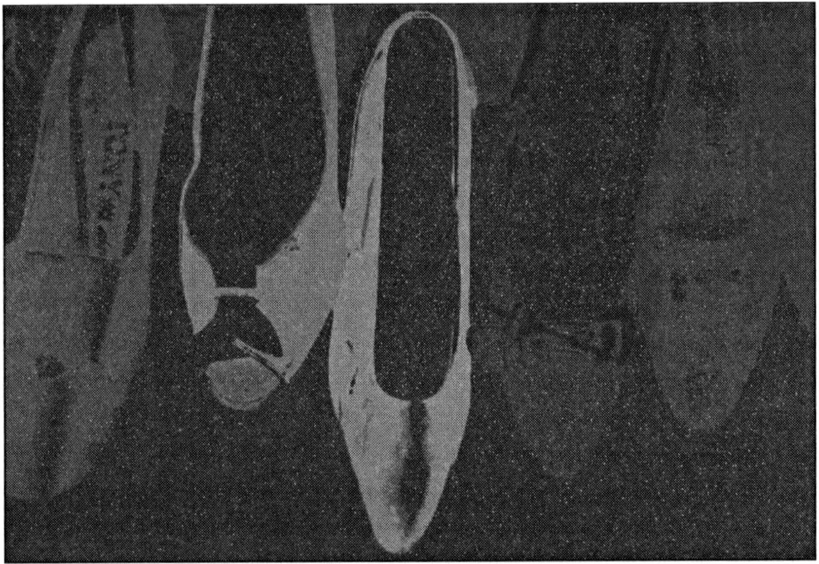

Figure 8. *Diamond Dust Shoes*, F&S 257, one from a portfolio of five screenprints with diamond dust printed on D'Arches Watercolor, by Andy Warhol, 1980. Hung upside down.

As in his van Gogh–Heidegger analysis, Jameson is indifferent, in his reading of Warhol, to the question of the painting, the specific painting to which he refers. Apparently, under the name of *Diamond Dust Shoes*, any Warhol shoe painting will do, any one from the 1980 Still Life series serves Jameson equally well: for the cover of *Postmodernism or, the Cultural Logic of Late Capitalism* features an illustration of one of Warhol's 1980 silkscreen prints, while the plate inside the book shows another, the latter, by the way, hung upside down (a Jamesonian "inversion of van Gogh's Utopian gesture" [9], a fetishizing of the shoe(s), once a being-erect, now impotently drooping?). This indifference to the particularity of the artwork seems to me to stage the very commodity fetishism that Jameson denounces in postmodern practice. The commodification of art that he diagnoses in Warhol, the reduction of the artwork to a useful object, a reified and reproducible end product, is modeled by Jameson's own appropriation of painting for its political and metaphysical use value, his treatment of the artwork as subsidiary, the implied interchangeability of artworks (one fetish object is a good as another). The painting itself is accessory or ornamental in Jameson's account, although the deflation of art into ornament is, for him, a lamentable feature of postmodern practice.[7]

On this note, I will turn to Derrida's "Restitutions," a good specimen of what Jameson calls "theory," since (coming out of France) it is not the propositional, dialectical discourse of an upright male subject, but a cut-up (contrapuntal) text written in inserts as a polylogue for n + 1 female voices. With its insistence on the question of *posting*—"Where do the shoes start from, to where and to whom do they return, from where do they return as they get closer, etc.?" (TP 357)—"Restitutions" challenges the aesthetics of interiority and self-proximity. Painted shoes cannot be put on the feet of an identifiable subject, Derrida maintains. What is more, shoes worn "*do not start out*, or at least don't go very far, and are already back" (366). For Derrida, if there is to be communication, a "voice" that is heard by someone other than me, words, like shoes, have to travel.

THE SCHAPIRO-HEIDEGGER CORRESPONDENCE

> The disparateness or the unevenness is that *there is* always one shoe more, or less: a third one or a first one.
>
> —Derrida, *The Truth in Painting*

"Restitutions of the truth in pointing [*pointure*]" takes as its pretext a 1968 essay by Meyer Schapiro, "The Still Life as a Personal Object— A Note on Heidegger and van Gogh." Schapiro's essay is dedicated to the memory of his friend, Kurt Goldstein, who first called his attention to Heidegger's *The Origin of the Work of Art*, the text with which Schapiro now takes bitter issue. By dedicating his essay to Goldstein, "Schapiro discharges a debt and a duty of friendship," Derrida says (TP 271). He also settles a political score. For Heidegger's artisanal pathos in *The Origin* is not unrelated, for Schapiro, to the Nazi ideology that forced Goldstein to flee Germany in 1933 and, after stops in Amsterdam and Paris, to emigrate in 1936 to New York and to Columbia University, where Schapiro was already teaching. "Schapiro bitterly disputes possession of the shoes with Heidegger, with 'Professor Heidegger,' who is seen then, all in all, to have tried to put them on his own feet, by peasant-proxy," Derrida suggests; "to put them *back* onto his man-of-the-soil feet, with the pathos of the 'call of the earth,' of the *Feldweg* or the *Holzwege* which, in 1935–6, was not foreign to what drove Goldstein to undertake his long march toward New York, via Amsterdam" (TP 272–73).[8] Derrida says that there is, then, "much to discharge, to return, to restitute" in the Schapiro-Heidegger debate over shoes; indeed, that it looks as if Schapiro, "not content with thanking a dead man for what he gave him to read," would offer to his memory "a detached part, a severed ear, but detached or severed from whom?" (273).[9]

From van Gogh (and by implication, from Schapiro himself). The painted shoes to which Heidegger refers in *The Origin of the Work of Art* are "the artist's own shoes, not the shoes of a peasant," Schapiro maintains (Schapiro 1968, 205). Schapiro does not doubt that the shoes form a pair. His concern is to establish that the pair belongs to the painter van Gogh, "as things inseparable from his body and memorable to his reacting self-awareness" (207). Schapiro comes to this conclusion only after corresponding with Heidegger by mail in 1965 and learning thereby that the van Gogh painting that Heidegger mentions in *The Origin* is one he saw in Amsterdam in March 1930. "This is clearly la Faille's no. 255," Schapiro declares, now making his correspondence with Heidegger public. Rather than expressing "the being or essence of a peasant woman's shoes and her relation to nature and work," these are undoubtedly "the shoes of the artist, by that time a man of the town and the city" (205). *Heidegger is wrong*, Schapiro insists:

> Alas for him, the philosopher has indeed deceived himself. He has retained from his encounter with van Gogh's canvas a moving set of associations with peasants and the soil, which are not sustained by the picture itself but are grounded rather in his own social outlook with its heavy pathos of the primordial and earthy. He has indeed "imagined everything and projected it into the painting." He has experienced both too little and too much in his contact with the work. (206)

Derrida does not simply disagree with Schapiro. Indeed, Heidegger's celebrated passage on the "famous picture by van Gogh" is, Derrida suggests, "ridiculous and lamentable" (TP 292), heavy with pathos, naïve in its recourse to an aesthetics of representation, "disappointing" in every way:

> So it really was the naïvete of what Schapiro rightly calls a "projection." One is not only disappointed when his [Heidegger's]

high academic seriousness, his severity and rigor of tone give way to this "illustration" (*bildliche Darstellung*). One is not only disappointed by the consumerlike hurry toward the content of representation, by the heaviness of the pathos, by the coded triviality of this description, which is both overloaded and impoverished, and one never knows if it's busying itself around a picture, "real" shoes, or shoes that are imaginary but outside painting; not only disappointed by the crudeness of the framing, the arbitrary and barbaric nature of the cutting-out, the massive self-assurance of the identification: "a pair of peasant shoes," just like that! Where did he get that from? Where does he explain himself on this matter? So one is not only disappointed, one sniggers. The fall in tension is too great. One follows step by step the moves of a "great thinker," as he returns to the origin of the work of art and of truth, traversing the whole history of the West, and then suddenly, at a bend in a corridor, here we are on a guided tour, as schoolchildren or tourists. Someone's gone to fetch the guide from the neighboring farm. Full of goodwill. He loves the earth and a certain type of painting when he can find himself in it [*quand il s'y retrouve*]. (292–93)[10]

But neither does Derrida agree with Schapiro, whose attribution of the shoes to the painter is no less problematic than Heidegger's alleged identification of them as the shoes of a peasant. For not only does Schapiro see the painting as a pair of "real shoes" that belong to a specifiable subject, he also returns the shoes to the signatory of the painting, who is here supposedly representing his own shoes or even himself in them. "Schapiro will see the 'face' [*la figure*] of van Gogh in 'his' shoes," Derrida writes (TP 266). Schapiro's interpretation constitutes the work's signature as a frame and its signatory as the subject of the canvas (the signed painting would be a self-portrait, in Schapiro's words, "a piece from a self-portrait" [1968, 207]).[11] Schapiro makes the canvas, in turn, into a foundation-frame, a structural support (a pair of "*subject*-shoes" [TP, 266]) used to hold up the subject, "the erect body in its contact with the ground" (Schapiro 1968, 207). Perhaps Schapiro, in returning the shoes to the signatory of the painting, outdoes Heidegger then; but in any case, both of the parties to this debate attach the shoes to a subject, a city-dweller on the one hand, a peasant on the other. Moreover, for both of these interpreters of art, the subject to whom the shoes are returned is "as close as can be to themselves, apparently" (TP 266).

This shared desire for restitution of the shoes to a subject (to oneself) constitutes a correspondence in difference, a pairing-together in the difference of opinion, between Heidegger and Schapiro, Derrida suggests. The fetish is the stake of the pair. For both Schapiro and Heidegger appropriate art for use, for its *usefulness* in presenting the truth of the subject.[12] And it is the truth of the subject that requires tight attachment of the shoes to their identified owner, as what Schapiro calls "things inseparable from his body" (Schaprio 1968, 207).[13] The desire for restitution "is a desire for appropriation. In matters of art as it is everywhere else" (TP 260). Involved in this intersection of the economic with the sexual fetish is an institution, a "tacit institution" (TP 282), Derrida says: "*restitution* reestablishes in rights or property by placing the subject upright again, in its stance, in its institution" (261). In its *teaching* institution: this is a debate between "great European university professors" (279) who have something to say about the hierarchical structure of the pedagogical institution that is erected in/on the painted shoes. Hence, the "high academic seriousness" (292) of Heidegger's tone in the passage on the painting, this alongside the art specialist, Schapiro's, peremptory precision in denouncing his opponent as, clearly and evidently, wrong. Considering that he has not read Heidegger's work, not even, Derrida suggests, all of *The Origin of the Work of Art*, Schapiro's posturing is particularly hard to take. Despite his academic courtesy and decorous references to "Professor Heidegger," Schapiro presents his case as if he were prosecuting at a restitution trial. "So Schapiro, insouciant, lays a trap for Heidegger," Derrida writes; "all the causes of this trial will have been traps" (276) laid in advance, and with all the righteous certainty of a verdict already won. "You can hear the noise: clear. It's clear, 'clearly' understood, the case has been heard, la Faille's 255, that can't come down/back to peasanthood: 'They are the shoes of the artist, by that time a man of the town and city.' *Hearing over*" (276, emphasis mine). Derrida is surprised by such "dogmatic and precritical language," Schapiro's *loud* repetitions of the words *evidently* and *clearly*: "It all looks as though the hammering of the notions of self-evidence, clarity, and property was meant to resound very loudly to prevent us from hearing that nothing here is clear, or self-evident, or proper to anyone of anything whatsoever" (313).

The language of clarity and visible immediacy suggests yet another correspondence between Schapiro and Heidegger in this exchange, one that puts both professors in agreement with Fredric Jameson: *the painted shoes talk*—to those who can hear (see) what they say. Both Schapiro and Heidegger make the artwork *speak*: "for both of them it's quite certain that the thing speaks," that "(Once they are painted,) these shoes talk" (TP 323).[14] Insofar as, in talking, the shoes restitute truth, return truth to the university's professor-subject, bind it close-to-himself, they cut off the ear of the other and institute the silence of *hearing-oneself-speak*. If the painted shoes are a self-portrait, then, as all three interpreters suggest, the portrait, in keeping with my reading of the Medusa effect, must be bandaged, a "bandaged self-portrait, the head wrapped up, pressed tightly in a bandage, hiding this time the missing part, but at the same time, exhibiting *in absentia* the lost 'personal object.' A curious still life" (360).

But what does "speak" mean to these interpreters of painting? "And speak *in painting*: truth spoken *itself*, as one says 'in painting'?" (TP 282), Derrida asks, as if mulling over a confusion of boundaries. Does painting actually speak, is truth actually spoken *in painting*, in the domain of painting rather than in an interpretive discourse, or is to speak *in painting* "only a manner of speaking, a figure—*painted*" (282), as it were, by these verbal interpretations of art? What Derrida alludes to here is not just a crossing of discourse and painting, the verbal and visual domains, although such crossing would already traverse the artwork's inside/outside frame. It would suggest that the relation between artwork and commentary "is one of interaction, rather than of hierarchy" (Bal 1991, 40), and thus that the artwork does not simply, usefully, speak an interpreter's truth. Such crossing would already call for another kind of pedagogy than is modeled in this debate: more critical, less haughty.[15]

With his reference to speech as a figure painted, Derrida is alluding to something else, however, something that Schapiro, with all his "simplifications" (TP 295),[16] is unaware of in *The Origin of the Work of Art*, something that introduces dissymmetry to the conformity that characterizes this debate over shoes. This something, Derrida says, has "to be thought of *in laces*" (TP 324) that cross the frame in both directions at once; an interlacing effect rather than an oppositional chop-cut. Most of "Restitutions," its one hundred and twenty-seven-some pages, explores this interlacing movement in *The Origin of the Work of Art.* "Restitutions," we might say, "returns slowly" (265) to *The Origin,* to the passage on van Gogh's painting but also to other "out-of-use places" (265) in the essay that Schapiro's reading either oversimplifies or omits. What matters to Derrida is that these out-of-the-way places change the structure of Heidegger's discourse, make his text *parergonal,* a matter of both being-in and being-out.

The glove is another figure of this in-and-out, and one that helps Derrida explain what he takes to be the psychoanalytic "truth" of the fetish, and of the fetishism of the shoe. According to Freud in his 1927 essay on "Fetishism," Derrida points out, the shoe, as substitute, would be "a 'form' of prosthesis, but always as a penis and a woman's penis. Detachable and reattachable" (TP 267). At the same time, however, in his *Introductory Lectures,* Freud classifies the shoe and the slipper as symbols of the female genital organs, and Ferenczi, too, sometimes sees a vagina in the shoe (267).

> In any case, *the* shoe, for Freud, is no more the penis than it is the vagina. Of course he recalls, against Steckel, that certain symbols cannot be *at the same time* both masculine and feminine. Of course he specifies that long, firm objects (weapons, for example) could not symbolize female genital organs, nor hollow objects (cases, boxes, coffers) masculine organs. But he does so only to admit immediately afterwards that bisexual symbolization remains an irrepressible, archaic tendency, going back to childhood which is ignorant of the difference of the sexes (*Traumdeutung,* VI, V). "Let us add here that most dream-symbols are bisexual and can, according to the circumstances, be referred to the organs of both sexes" (*Über den Traum*). According to the circumstances, in other words also according to a syntax irreducible to any semantic or "symbolic" substantiality. (268)

According to Derrida, then, the shoe, in psychoanalysis, suggests not either masculinity or femininity so much as "bisexuality," and/or a movement *between* one and the other. "Could it be that, like a glove turned inside out, the shoe sometimes has the convex 'form' of the foot (penis), and sometimes the concave form enveloping the foot (vagina)?" (267). Not only in Freud, but also in *The Origin of the Work of Art*, Derrida ventures, the shoe, like a glove, will be what turns the inside out and brings the outside in. One might begin to read *The Origin* with this back-and-forth movement in mind, always "hold[ing] in reserve a sort of excess of interpretation, a supplement of reading" and refraining from "ready-to-wear" or "off-the-peg universals" (268) of the sort that Schapiro proposes. And although this is a debate about shoes, and about laces tied and untied, one might begin by recalling that, in Heidegger's texts, this in-and-out gives the movement of language: "This place which I begin by occupying slowly, before the race, can here only be a place of language" (263).

Because it is this in-and-out, "this *strophe* of the lace" (TP 299), that Derrida reads in *The Origin*, and that can be felt in turn in the movement between the n + 1 voices of "Restitutions," a different sense of hearing emerges from Derrida's essay than the *hearing-oneself-speak* that has characterized the shoe debate thus far. Derrida in "Restitutions" makes no claim to see or to hear a truth internal to the frame. He enters the Schapiro-Heidegger debate, he says, not to join the fight over shoes.[17] "Nobody's being accused, or above all condemned, or even suspected. *There is* painting, writing, restitutions, that's all" (371). As was the case in the previous chapter, Derrida's reading of Heidegger here involves his tracking of *the path* (*la marche, la marque*) of certain words or figures in Heidegger's text, the word become path, the figure figuring the rhythm of language, its pulsing on—imprinting of—the tympan (canvas, membrane, surface, skin).[18] Derrida, we might say, is interested in the path trekked out by shoes in *The Origin of the Work of Art*, and not just when the shoes are put on the feet of a university professor. Here, as in Derrida's reading of Kant in chapter 2, the way in which, in an "academic" text, walking shoes—and left and right feet—come into contact with the ground, bears directly on the matter of institutional foundations, the basic supports that the founding text in question constructs as the university's footings. The shoes *as institution* are always in play in "Restitutions," in its word play, for instance, in the back-and-forth movement this play inscribes between different senses. For Derrida, to read Heidegger's *The Origin of the Work of Art* as a text about university footings means "following the figure or trajectory of the *lace*: a stricture by alternate and reversible passage from inside to outside, from under to over" (321).[19] Without taking account of—without hearing—this lacing movement in *The Origin*, he says, "there is no chance of understanding anything in these pages on 'the famous picture,' no chance of making the slightest objection that could be pertinently measured against them" (352).

Since laces, and interlacing, are so much at issue in Derrida's reading, we might take a look ourselves here at the laces van Gogh painted in his shoes, particularly in la Faille's no. 255, the painting that Schapiro insists Heidegger is discussing in *The Origin of the Work of Art*. Schapiro reproduces this painting in his essay under the title "Old Shoes." In "Restitutions," Derrida reproduces the same painting as "Old Shoes with Laces." Considering this discrepancy, Derrida explains that he takes his title from "the large catalog of the Tuileries exhibition (1971–2) (collection of the Vincent van Gogh National Museum in Amersterdam)" (TP 276). Derrida does "not yet know how much is due to van Gogh in the choice of this title" (276), however, and so says he is prepared to leave the matter of the correct

Figure 9. A *Pair of Shoes*, F 255, oil on canvas, by Vincent van Gogh, Paris, 1886. Amsterdam, van Gogh Museum.

title in suspense, "as a certain essential indeterminacy forms part of our problem which is also the problem of the title" (276).[20] Yet there is obviously something of significance for Derrida in Schapiro's cutting of the laces out of the title "Old Shoes." Indeed, playing on the double meaning of *lacet* in French, both shoelace and snare (and the lace in Faille 255 does take the shape of a snare), Derrida suggests that the laces have to do with a trap, the one that Schapiro lays for Heidegger "before catching his own feet in it" (275). The laces constitute a trap inasmuch as they induce Schapiro to tie the shoes together so as to make them into a pair, a pair of real shoes that are in turn tied to the feet of their author-subject ("he takes them back, with a 'they're mine' ['*it's coming back to me;*' *ça me revient*]" [260]). But in la Faille's no. 255, Derrida notes, the painted shoelaces are actually untied, and the shoes themselves are unloosed from each other, "detached, by this fact, one from the other and nothing proves that they form a pair" (277). Nothing proves that the shoes belong on the feet of the speaking subject—that truth is the university's, or the professor's, property. The shoes are unattached, and their laces are also undone, almost adrift, as if untied from the feet of a *being-upright* as well as from the ground of a *being-underneath*. In all his haste to claim the painted shoes that he maintains Heidegger is discussing, Schapiro, it seems, overlooks the painting itself, the laces painted loose, unattached and untied. He also misses the ways in which a trajectory of lacing marks *The Origin of the Work of Art.*

Derrida suggests that Heidegger may also have overlooked the painting himself, or at least, that when he is discussing the example of a pair of peasant shoes, Heidegger is not necessarily referring to any picture at all. In a discussion that goes on for several pages of *The Origin,* no picture is necessary, and none, Derrida notes, is invoked— for Heidegger's discourse in those pages concerns something external to a picture frame, and external to the frame of this debate: the being-product of shoes. It is possible, Derrida says, that up to, and even including, the infamous passage, Heidegger does not intend to speak of any picture at all, save as "the example of the example (some particular shoes in some particular picture)" (TP 319), in which case, the pictorial limit belongs not to Heidegger but to Schapiro. Derrida suggests that there are several instances in *The Origin* where Heidegger's discussion of the shoes, like a glove, overflows the frame, inside-out and/or outside-in, and so raises the issue of the limit—and its crossing—perhaps the main issue in this debate, even if Schapiro altogether neglects it. Such crossing, at crucial places in *The Origin*— where the product-status of shoes and sexual determination are concerned—results in an indeterminacy that makes it difficult, more difficult than Schapiro suggests, to pin Heidegger down to a consistent discourse on truth. Indeed, in Derrida's reading, no sooner does Heidegger approach the truth in painting, than his discourse falls short of it by passing outside of the picture into discussion of an *hors-d'oeuvre* (307). No sooner does Heidegger engage a discourse of representation by attaching shoes to a peasant,[21] than he unties the shoes from a subject (as also from "real" shoes) and exceeds a representational frame. Heidegger does not stop at the limit that separates inside from out, but in the movement of his discussion, he steps beyond the picture's edge, broaches the frame in both directions at once. As if he were holding "the thing, the shoes in painting, by the lace and play[ing] with the bobbin" (357), he both draws toward the truth of representation and lets truth go away. He both chooses the painting as useful for his purposes and abandons it, "lets the picture drop like an old shoe" (328). *Passing through* the process of fetishization, at once gathering back to the truth of the fetish, sexual and economic, and interrupting the moment of presence, "lacing across the line in both directions, making come back, making go away, making come back again, inside, outside, down there, here, *fort, da*" (357), Heidegger's discourse snares and sets loose, ties and unties, attaches and unbinds. It thereby *figures* a back-and-forth, inside-outside trajectory of the lace. The interlace, in turn, is *The Origin's*—painted—*figure of speech*, of the way that truth speaks in painting.[22]

REST(E)S OF THE TRUTH IN PAINTING

Then, let's get back into the classroom.

—Derrida, *The Truth in Painting*

Insofar as Heidegger, in *The Origin of the Work of Art*, locates truth *in* painting, he confines pedagogical and institutional footings to the oppositional binaries I have been so critical of in this book—binaries that, as I argue in the previous chapter, are at the center of the insidious politics of the so-called Heidegger affair; binaries that cut off the university's ear for the other in favor of the autoaffective, phonocentric *hearing-oneself-speak*. Although he differentiates his own position from Heidegger's, and, implicitly at least, for reasons that link to Heidegger's politics, Schapiro's reading of the shoes confines us to these binaries as well. This is the "pairing of a correspondence" (TP 257), this is the "common code" (279), that Derrida identifies in the Schapiro-Heidegger debate: the reciprocal recognition by both parties of the pair, and the attachment of the pair to the feet of their owner. For Derrida, both Schapiro and Heidegger contract in truth, and to the extent that they do, both offer politically fraught discourses on painting, discourses that are haunted by "an army of ghosts [who] are demanding their shoes. Ghosts up in arms, an immense tide of deportees searching for their names. If you want to go to this theatre, here's the road of affect: the bottomless memory of a dispossession, an expropriation, a despoilment. And there are tons of shoes piled up there, pairs mixed up and lost" (329–31). It is not insignificant that neither of the disputants addresses these ghosts. On this matter, both share a common code of silence.

What haunts calls for response. What needs to be addressed, according to Derrida, is the limit that this binary logic sets up. *The Origin* is not free of the binaries of metaphysics. But at the same time, in several of its motifs, in the trajectory of several of the figures that Derrida follows, Heidegger's argumentation is not reducible, as Schapiro would have it, to an oppositional chop/cut/slash. What it suggests, rather, in its lacing movement "from inside to outside, from outside to inside" (301), in its *fort/da* "play of appearance/disappearance" (304), is a *trait* on/as the frame, thus always already a broaching, "already a tracing of coming and going between the outside and the inside" (303).[23] For reason of this movement, I have approached Heidegger's writing, in this and the previous chapter, as, for Derrida, something of a hinge. Derrida uses the word *hinge* (*charnière*) himself, in a discussion of what Freud's work means to Foucault. "Why a *charnière*? This word can be taken in the technical or anatomical sense of a central or cardinal articulation, a hinge pin (*cardo*) or pivot. A *charnière* or hinge is an axial device that enables the circuit, the trope, or the movement of rotation" (R 78). Like the lever, the leverage of the foot, that would enable Kant's infantryman to swing onto his horse, the leverage that would take his university across the medieval-to-modern divide, a hinge is what enables movement, what gives swing across the frame: "[t]his double articulation, this double movement or alternation between opening and closing that is assured by the work-ings of a hinge, this coming and going: indeed this *fort/da* play of a pendulum [*pendule*] or balance [*balancier*]" (78). I am tempted, by these terms, to consider each ear ossicle as a hinge, the back-and-forth movement of which enables sound (and shoes) to travel. Insofar as Heidegger allows the *os* to vibrate, and so to imprint a tympanum, he would be for Derrida, as is Freud for Foucault, "the doorman of the today, the holder of the keys, of those that open as well as those that close the door" (79). Heidegger, in Derrida's reading, "both stands guard and ushers in"; he simultaneously "closes one epoch" in the philosophy of the research university and "opens another"(79).

I will close this chapter and open onto the next with a passing comment on the idea of another, call it "postmodern," institution—its form and its footings. I am thinking of Derrida's remark in "Res-titutions" that the more he looks at the shoes in la Faille's no. 255, "the less they look like an old pair" (TP 278). In fact, considering "the details, the inside lateral surface: you'd think it was two left feet. Of different shoes" (278). What kind of footing would such a hybrid

Figure 10. Nunotani Corporation Headquarters Building, Tokyo, Japan, 1990–1992. Exterior view from northeast. Eisenman Architects.

pair provide? Can a university stand, *erect*, on two left feet, or might it be a body that "squints or limps," to use Derrida's words from "Restitutions" (265)?[24] I'll rest on these questions, and on one remaining image. Since I move, in the next chapter, to an institutional, architectural, collaboration between Derrida and Peter Eisenman, I have taken the image from Eisenman's work, his 1992 Nunotani Office Building in Tokyo, Japan. Since the land mass of Japan is subject to earthquake activity, the building is designed to receive the waves that pass through it; in Eisenman's words, the building is "a metaphoric record of these continuous waves of movement" (Eisenman 1995, 178). Simultaneously, the project represents an attempt to rethink the vertical institution, "first by producing a building that is not metaphorically skeletal or striated, but rather made up of a shell of vertically compressed and translated plates; and second, by producing an image somewhere *between* an erect and a 'limp' condition" (178, my emphasis).

SIX

ARCHITECTURE'S (THE UNIVERSITY'S) *CHORA*: TWO POSTMODERN COLLABORATIONS

What survives deconstruction must have new forms.

—Derrida, "On Colleges and Philosophy"

MARK WIGLEY REMINDS US in *The Architecture of Deconstruction* that institutions "are built in and by discourse" (Wigley 1993, 51). With this in mind, I have been reading several philosophers of the university as architects of sorts. I do the same in the following chapter, which begins by positioning the philosopher as architect. The philosopher in question is Paul Ricoeur. His 1975 study *La Métaphore vive*, translated in 1977 as *The Rule of Metaphor*, presents an argument that, I argue, has an architecture in it, an architecture that is consistent with Kant's hierarchical inside/outside, *ergon/parergon* university design. Ricoeur's study takes issue with Derrida's, and deconstruction's, "orientation" on metaphor—again, for structural and architectural reasons that have to do with the university's grounding and elevation, and with the disciplines and their interrelations. The very question of the institution's life and death is said to be at stake in this debate over the meaning of metaphor, and over metaphor as meaning; the life-or-death question introduces a biological metaphor to the metaphor debate, and this in turn leads to the specter of a body with its animating member cut off. Ricoeur makes the case, against deconstruction,

111

Figure 11. Parc de la Villette, Paris, France. Bernard Tschumi Architects. Photograph J. M. Monthiers

for reattachment of the *animus*. I will suggest that, like the argument for reattachment of the shoes, Ricoeur's is a case for a returning to the spirit-self of metaphysics, and therefore, to the silence/silencing of *hearing-oneself-speak*.

Alongside the reading of Ricoeur, the philosopher-as-architect, the first part of this chapter reads an architect, Alberto Pérez-Gómez, as a kind of philosopher. His "*Chora*: The Space of Architectural Representation," which is a history and philosophy of *the* architectural metaphor *chora*, works out of assumptions similar to Ricoeur's, and it presents a similar university design, one that, in Pérez-Gómez's terminology, would be called "postmodern." Taking the word *chora* from Plato's *Timaeus*, Pérez-Gómez moves in his discussion of metaphor, as does Ricoeur, to figures of embodiment, fecundity, birth, and the *animus*—the singing *choros* of men in Greek theatre—to which he opposes the death-dealing, dismembering, architecture of today's technological world. I will suggest, however, that the poetic-metaphoric *saying* that, for Pérez-Gómez, restores voice and life to architecture, and to its structures, is in service of a *logos* that, traditionally at least, disembodies speech and ear.

The second part of this chapter deals with another philosophy-architecture collaboration, this one between Derrida and Peter Eisenman. Also a work on metaphor, and on Plato's metaphor *chora* in particular, this collaboration involved the joint design of a garden for Bernard Tschumi's Parc de la Villette in Paris. One of Derrida's contributions to the project was his essay on the *Timaeus*, "*Chora*," on the basis of which Eisenman titled their project *Chora L Work*. I approach this work-in-concert as having to do primarily with the *imprinting* and *spacing movement* that can reembody hearing and the academic institution of the ear.

THE ART OF METAPHOR

> The term *vive* in the title of [*La Métaphore vive*] is all important, for it was my purpose to demonstrate that there is not just an epistemo-logical and political imagination, but also, and perhaps more fundamentally, a linguistic imagination which generates and regener-ates meaning through the living power of metaphoricity.
>
> —Ricoeur, *Reflection and Imagination*

> Kantian question: the relation of the concept to the nonconcept (up/down, left/right), to the body, to the signature which is placed "on" the frame: in fact, sometimes; structurally, always.
>
> —Derrida, *The Truth in Painting*

Paul Ricoeur's *The Rule of Metaphor* is a composition of four parts. The book begins with, and is grounded in, Aristotelian *rhetoric* since, as Ricoeur explains, Aristotle "actually defined metaphor for the entire subsequent history of Western thought" (Ricoeur 1977, 3), defined it as a semantic or meaning-making unit. But whereas Aristotle defines metaphor as a name or a word, Ricoeur's study, in its second moment, shifts theory of metaphor to what he calls a *semantics* of discourse, where the sentence, not the word, is the minimal metaphoric unit, the sentence in which a "semantic impertinence" or logical absurdity is put into effect.[1] Metaphor, as such a case of "impertinent predica-tion," results in semantic innovation, the interpretation of which, Ricoeur explains in the third moment of his study, requires the pas-sage from semantics to *hermeneutics*. Specifically, Ricoeur's theory of metaphor requires a hermeneutics of poetic reference, an approach that allows for the (dialectical) suspension of literal reference as the condition for release of higher, second-degree, metaphorical truth. With this incursion into the problematic of truth, poetry reaches its limit, and Ricoeur's study enters its final *philosophical* stage. In this final passage, charted through the Aristotelian doctrine of analogy, poetry gives place to, and gives way to, philosophy and the speculative *logos*.

That *The Rule of Metaphor* moves through these four moments—rhetoric, semantics, hermeneutics, philosophy—is in itself indicative of the book's reliance on Aristotelian thought. For in order to talk about metaphor, Aristotle himself created a metaphor, carried over from the realm of movement, *phora*, "a kind of change, namely change with respect to location," Ricoeur explains (Ricoeur 1977, 17). Aristotle's *epiphora* characterizes metaphor as movement. And because his rhetoric is "solidly bound to philosophy" (10), Aristotle directs the movement in a certain way, in the same way that Ricoeur directs it in his study—from poetry to philosophy—even as, in determining this directional movement, Aristotle (also Ricoeur) establishes a necessary hierarchy between metaphor (poetry) and philosophy: a relation that, while it links the two, requires that poetry yield to philosophy in each and every case. For to theorize metaphor as semantic gain cannot be to intrude on philosophy's conceptual domain. Ricoeur maintains that "speculative discourse has its condition of *possibility* in the semantic dynamism of metaphorical utterance," but at the same time, that "speculative discourse has its *necessity* in itself" (296). The function of metaphorical discourse, what, following Aristotle, gives poetry-as-metaphor its privileged status, is its *semantic* creativity, its production, through what Ricoeur calls a metaphorical *twist*, of *new meaning*. But this increase in meaning is "not yet a *conceptual* gain" (296), not, at least, until poetry gives way to philosophy, not until the passage to philosophy is complete. The order of the four moments of his study—rhetoric, semantics, hermeneutics, philosophy—must not be reversed, then, for the order gives the direction in which metaphor as *epiphora*, transpositional movement, proceeds, the direction *from . . . to*, from poetry to philosophy, from metaphor to the concept.[2]

There is an architecture, a university architecture, in this argument, in this positioning (by a philosopher) of philosophy as an uppermost endpoint: as origin (the horizon of the speculative *logos*,

Ricoeur says, is given "in advance" [Ricoeur 1977, 302]); as ground (the speculative is "first discourse in the order of grounding" [300]); and, although it receives semantic input from metaphor, as wholly autonomous where concepts, and the language/*logos* of concepts, are concerned ("That speculative discourse finds something like the sketch of a conceptual determination in the dynamism [of metaphor] does not bar it from beginning in itself and from finding the principle of its articulation within itself. By itself" [300]). The resources of speculative philosophy, Ricoeur says, are those of "the mind itself reflecting upon itself" (296), a contention that is consistent with the Kantian-Hegelian schema, the *hearing-oneself-speak* schema, I have been examining in this book. In the process of confirming the traditional hierarchy of the philosophical over the literary disciplines, Ricoeur's argument inevitably redraws certain inside/outside lines, suggesting what is intrinsic and necessary to philosophy—and poetry—proper, and what is extraneous, unnecessary, and even dangerous to these. It is his particular concern to argue that metaphor, metaphorical utterance, is about semantic gain and not stylistic ornament. A metaphor is not a word, Ricoeur insists: indeed, it's "the tyranny of the word in the theory of meaning" that has led to the "error" of "the reduction of metaphor to a mere ornament" (45), an "ornament of discourse" (Ricoeur 1976, 52). Only as emergent meaning can metaphor provide the crucial (institutional) poetry-to-philosophy bridge. This structural link is the contribution of Aristotle's original rhetoric. As a threefold discipline that included argumentation, composition, and style, Aristotle's founding rhetoric was firmly tied to philosophy, even as it stood under philosophy's "watchful eye" (Ricoeur 1977, 12). Indeed, Aristotle's rhetoric was not only an integral whole, a rational construction in its own right, but also the structural link on which "the whole edifice of a philosophy was constructed" (12). Only later, when rhetoric was restricted to style and then to a theory of ornamental tropes and so to a "taxonomy of figures of speech" (10), was the connection between poetry and philosophy broken. Rhetoric "lost the nexus that bound it through dialectic to philosophy" (10), and with that, "the destiny of metaphor [was] sealed for centuries to come" (14).

As if dis-aggregation of the Aristotelian foundation were also an historical and institutional dis-orientation, a matter of errant destiny or destination, Ricoeur situates his theory of metaphor within a narrative of fragmentation and loss. In his account, no less than life and death are at stake in the historical decline of Aristotelian rhetoric. He refers to Aristotle's triadic rhetoric as an organic whole, a living body that died when its crucial, animating, member, argumentation, was cut off, eventually leaving behind only an emasculated ornament, mere style ("decoration," "delectation"). Today, Aristotle's rhetoric is "not merely defunct but amputated as well," Ricoeur claims (1977, 9). "Rhetoric died when the penchant for classifying figures of speech completely supplanted the philosophical sensibility that animated the vast empire of rhetoric, held its parts together and tied the whole to the *organon* and to first philosophy"(10).[3] The "dismembering" is what Ricoeur deplores, and is what fills him with a "sense of irremediable loss" (10). His approach is "completely opposed to any reduction of metaphor to a mere 'ornament'" (22).[4] For him, metaphor must be thought of as a "work in miniature" (Ricoeur 1981, 167), as a discursive event of meaning-making. Originally, rhetoric, the art of persuasion, would have belonged to a speech-act situation that, as Ricoeur has it, "directly connects the voice of one to the hearing of another" (147). While writing, in his argument, is supposed to have taken the place of speech and its semantic–heuristic immediacy, the written text, and metaphor as a miniature of this, is still considered to be fulfilled "in speech" and restored "to living communication" (152) only when it is interpreted as meaning. This reanimation of the text is impossible in post-Saussurian linguistic theory (which Ricoeur refers to as a "semiotic monism" [Ricoeur 1977, 102]), where metaphor, he says, is reduced to a word, a sign, and where the text is approached solely in terms of relations between its constituent units. This is an analysis of poststructuralist linguistics that pertains to written texts, but it is nonetheless a narrative of the disabled *os*, of the loss, in current theory, of the kind of interpretation in which "reading becomes like speech" (Ricoeur 1981, 159).

It is emphatically the case that when Ricoeur looks at "deconstruction," he sees this disabled, speechless *os*, an Aristotelian body that has been amputated (castrated), deprived of its life-giving member. In deconstruction, which, according to him, unfolds as an unbroken development from Heidegger to Derrida, "from Heidegger's restrained criticism" of philosophy of metaphor to "Jacques Derrida's unbounded 'deconstruction' in 'White Mythology'" (Ricoeur 1977, 284), Derrida's essay on metaphor ("White Mythology: Metaphor in the Text of Philosophy") in *Margins of Philosophy*,[5] metaphor is dealt a final, fatal blow. Derrida's work on metaphor "moves counter" (285) to his own, Ricoeur contends, and therefore it "reverse[s] the order of priority between metaphor and philosophy" (258). Derrida also "reverses the pattern of philosophical augmentation" (258–59), for rather than taking metaphor, metaphoric creativity, to be productive of new conceptual possibilities for philosophy as Aristotle did, Derrida's analysis of metaphor moves in the opposite direction, from philosophy to literary trope, from the concept to mere ornament or figure of speech.[6] With deconstruction, we "enter the domain of metaphor not by way of its birth but, if we may say so, by way of its death" (285). For instead of directing his analysis "towards the discovery of living metaphor" (285), as Ricoeur himself does, Derrida focuses on the unacknowledged prevalence of dead metaphors in metaphysics.[7] And not unrelated to this, Derrida's deconstructive operation dissects ("dismembers") the text, reducing metaphor to worn-out word and dismantling the difference between philosophy and figure. That Ricoeur misreads Derrida on each of these points, that he attributes to Derrida the very assertions that Derrida puts into question in "White Mythology," is a matter that Derrida deals with at length in "The *Retrait* of Metaphor." Suffice it to say that Ricoeur's anxiety about deconstruction is clear. Like Kant, he wants to keep the parasite, and the *parergon*, out. He wants to banish tropes to the outside of philosophy, including philosophy of metaphor. And like Kant, he warns, in strong terms, of the danger of bringing the outside in, of introducing figures where new meaning and new concepts should be. Derrida's work on metaphor is "only one episode in a much vaster strategy of deconstruction that always consists in destroying metaphysical discourse," Ricoeur says, and the conclusions of "White Mythology" are "scarcely more than one groundwork for an enterprise that foments a good many other subversive manoeuvres" (287).

Setting his own work against this perceived subversion, Ricoeur takes it as his task to revive metaphysics, here by way of his theory of living metaphor, *la métaphore vive*. Living metaphor conducts us to the threshold of philosophy's dwelling; indeed, Ricoeur says, metaphor's meaning has to do with possible modes of being-in-the-world displayed by a text, "a proposed world which I could inhabit and in which I could project my inmost possibilities" (Ricoeur 1981, 112). Such meaning, articulated through a metaphorical sense of the verb to be, *to be like* or *to be as*, provides the analogical link, the copula, between poetry and philosophy, ensuring that the like/as of analogy, the ana-, has semantic import and is not just the "pleasing adornment" (Ricoeur 1977, 247) of a figure of speech. On the other hand, the very tension or twist that produces the analogy also prevents poetry from entering philosophy's house. For although poetry allows for the dynamism of metaphor's tensive split-reference, speculative discourse works on the altogether different level of the concept, "free of interpretations, schematizations, and imaginative illustrations" (302). Philosophy's domain is beyond the order of images and perceptions of sense. As, following Ricoeur's movement *from . . . to*, we approach university's center, then, we must needs accede to "the quietness of the concept" (Ricoeur 1991, 125). When we reach the center, *epiphora*'s movement stops. *The Rule of Metaphor* thus comes to its end in an unmoving and uncanny silence—a situation that, I have said in earlier chapters of this book, effectively renders philosophy and its institution dumbstruck. Ricoeur's work on metaphor comes to its rest in the disembodied interiority of traditional metaphysics, thinking life itself as spirit, "the spirit (*Geist*)" that Kant calls "'the life-giving principle of mind (*Gemüt*)'" (Ricoeur 1977, 303). Just as for Kant, where understanding fails, "imagination forces conceptual thought to *think more*," so, Ricoeur says, "[m]etaphor is living to the extent that it vivifies a constituted language. Metaphor is living by virtue of the fact that it introduces the spark of imagination into a 'thinking more' at the conceptual level. This struggle to 'think more,' guided by the 'vivifying principle,' is the 'soul' of interpretation" (303; see also Ricoeur 1981, 53).[8]

Much the same conclusion is reached by architect Alberto Pérez-Gómez, for whom such "thinking more" is the appropriate task for architecture in the postmodern world. Just as there is an architecture in philosopher Paul Ricoeur's work on metaphor, so there is a philosophy in the architecture of Pérez-Gómez. Like Ricouer, Pérez-Gómez is interested in metaphor. Indeed, his essay "*Chora*: the Space of Architectural Representation" is a history and philosophy of metaphor, specifically of the metaphor *chora*, which he takes to be the preeminent figure of architecture as a fine art. I bring his work on metaphor together here with Ricoeur's as suggesting one type of contemporary philosophy-architecture collaboration, Pérez-Gómez would call it "postmodern." The goal of such collaboration would be to provide "an appropriate choreography for a postmodern world" (Pérez-Gómez 1994, 32), and for Pérez-Gómez, as for Ricoeur, the task would involve retrieval of the original Greek sense of wholeness. Like Ricouer, Pérez-Gómez, in his theorizing of metaphor, argues for recovery of an original, organic Greek vision of life; he also sets his analysis of contemporary approaches to metaphor, in this case *chora*, within an overall narrative of dismemberment and loss of this foundation.

According to Pérez-Gómez, it's the original Greek understanding of space that post-Renaissance Western culture collapsed, an originary sense of space that is best articulated by Plato in his discussion of *chora* in the *Timaeus*. The discussion in question centers on two accounts of the creation of the universe. In the first of these accounts, the Demiurge, architect of the cosmos, fashions the visible world as copy of an intelligible idea. To these two forms of reality, the intelligible and the sensible, Being and Becoming, Plato's second creation account adds another, *chora*, a term that he says is "difficult and obscure," but that can be described as "the receptacle and, as it were, the nurse of all becoming and change" (Plato 1965, 67), the place that receives the forms created by the Demiurge, while yet always remaining virgin. Plato compares the receptacle to the gold that a craftsman imprints with one shape or another, for like gold, *chora* "is a kind of neutral plastic material on which changing impressions are stamped by the things which enter it, making it appear different at different times" (69), although its reality remains the same, and it never becomes the copy with which it is inscribed. "We may indeed use the metaphor of birth and compare the receptacle to the mother, the model to the father, and what they produce between them to their offspring," Plato says (69). However, the third term, this mother and receptacle of visible and sensible things, is neuter and "devoid of all character" (70), thus "very hard to grasp" (70), apprehensible only "by a sort of spurious reasoning" (71). As if it were a "winnowing basket" or a "kind of shaking implement" that separates the four elements (fire, air, water, earth) out of itself, the receptacle "sway[s] unevenly" and is "in constant process of movement and separation" (72). What Pérez-Gómez takes from these passages is a definition of *chora* as, in architecture, a term for the "depth" dimension of a built structure, something that points beyond the work to a meaning, something that enables meaning, and therefore being, to increase. *Chora*, the third term, figures the new reality that is released, or realized, through the architectural—dialectical—crossing of the intelligible and sensible realms. *Chora* is the heuristic "epiphany" (Pérez-Gómez 1994, 14) that an architectural work occasions. It's akin to the transformative and life-renewing catharsis that took place in Greek theatre through the singing and poetic saying of the chorus of men who danced on the *chora*, the theatre platform. The reconciliation that this ritual catharsis effected, the higher-order realization of, and participation in, the wholeness of the universe, then became, says Pérez-Gómez, the paradigm for Western art and architecture.

As much as Ricoeur, Pérez-Gómez laments the loss of the Greek sense of wholeness in favor of modernity's scientific worldview, with its "objectification and enframing" and the "instrumental rationality" to which these have led (Pérez-Gómez 1994, 13). Architecture, as the art of space, the art of metaphor, the art of *chora*, has all but disappeared from today's instrumental and technological culture, where building is about the manipulation of objects and space—"an objectified *chora*" (24)—and about conforming to the technological values of efficiency and economy—as if meaning-making were not the architect's concern. "Early in the nineteenth century, the École des Beaux Arts attempted to temper this dangerous proximity to the task of the engineer through the recovery of architectural tradition, but the crucial question of the meaning of art for art's sake was not raised. In this context, architecture could only be the stylistic ornament attached to the shed" (26). Like Ricoeur, and like Kant before him, Pérez-Gómez defends metaphor—architecture as the art of *chora*—against the ornament. Like Ricoeur, in aligning architecture with poetry, with life-giving poetic speech, Pérez-Gómez puts metaphor in the service of traditional metaphysics. Only in such service, only in conducting us back to *Geist*, would architecture, according to Pérez-Gómez, be appropriately postmodern. The architect, in his postmodern world, would once again become a seer-poet informed by a Greek vision of wholeness; his designs, scripts for this vision, would be "the vehicle for an ethical intention to inform the work" (31); and his creations, his built structures, through their essential depth, would effect a disclosure, an "intensification" (30) of philosophical truth.

CHORA L

The stone still resonates and vibrates, it emits a kind of painful and indecipherable bliss, one no longer knows whose or for whom . . .

—Derrida, "Unsealing ('the old new language')," in *Points*

My suggestion is that in his analysis of architecture's *chora*, Pérez-Gómez, although he is an architect, leaves out the question of structure. Perhaps this is not surprising, for according to Derrida in his essay "*Chora*," the question of structure seems "never to have been approached as such by the whole history of the interpretations of the *Timaeus*" (CW 17), and this despite the fact that a "structural law," a "structural anachronism" (17), is very much at issue in Plato's text.[9] In "The *Retrait* of Metaphor," Derrida suggests that not only in interpretations of *chora*, but in work on metaphor overall, Ricoeur's included, this question of structure gets "left in the dark" (RM 17). With Derrida's writing on metaphor, however, even with the title word *retrait*, structure is always already in play.[10] And it is structure, a structural *retrait*, that makes metaphor's *epiphora*, for him, not simply a semantic transfer, certainly not a continuist one-way movement *from* poetry *to* the concept, but also, and more so, a matter of the coming-going *movement* of language itself, the kind of movement that a writer-speaker cannot control, let alone steer in one direction, the kind of movement that philosophy cannot integrate and sublate. We cannot treat of metaphor, Derrida says, "cannot *treat it* (*en traiter*) without *dealing with it* (*sans traiter avec elle*)" (7) on its own terms; not without dealing with the vibratory movement of what Heidegger called the *trait*. While for Ricoeur, metaphor's surplus is solely semantic, is ever-new meaning, the dialectical result of what he calls the metaphorical *twist*, for Derrida, metaphor's surplus, "always marking with a supplementary trait" (8), has as much to do with the "invaginated" or "twisted structure" (14) that language is, "the intractable structure in which we are implicated and deflected from the outset" (13).[11] This structure made futile Kant's, Hegel's, and Heidegger's attempts to separate outside from in; it frustrates Ricoeur's proposed bounding off of philosophy from poetry, his called-for giving-way of metaphor to concept. Derrida's *twist* is relevant to my study precisely because it is a figure of spacing, *espacement* (see Lawlor 1983, 330). And it is attention to spacing—the movement of metaphor, the movement of re-turn and withdrawal that leaves its *trait* in a text (*no hearing without movement, without an imprint of some sort*)—that distinguishes the second philosophy-architecture collaboration I want to introduce here, this one between Derrida and Peter Eisenman who, on the invitation of Bernard Tschumi, worked together on the design of a "garden" for the campus at Parc de la Villette .

The campus, as I choose to call it, including music and science centers, commercial offices and public open spaces, is located on a large 125 acre expanse in the northeast corner of Paris, a site previously occupied by the city's central slaughterhouses. Here, in 1983, after winning a design competition of more than 470 submissions from seventy countries, Tschumi began work on a dispersed building,

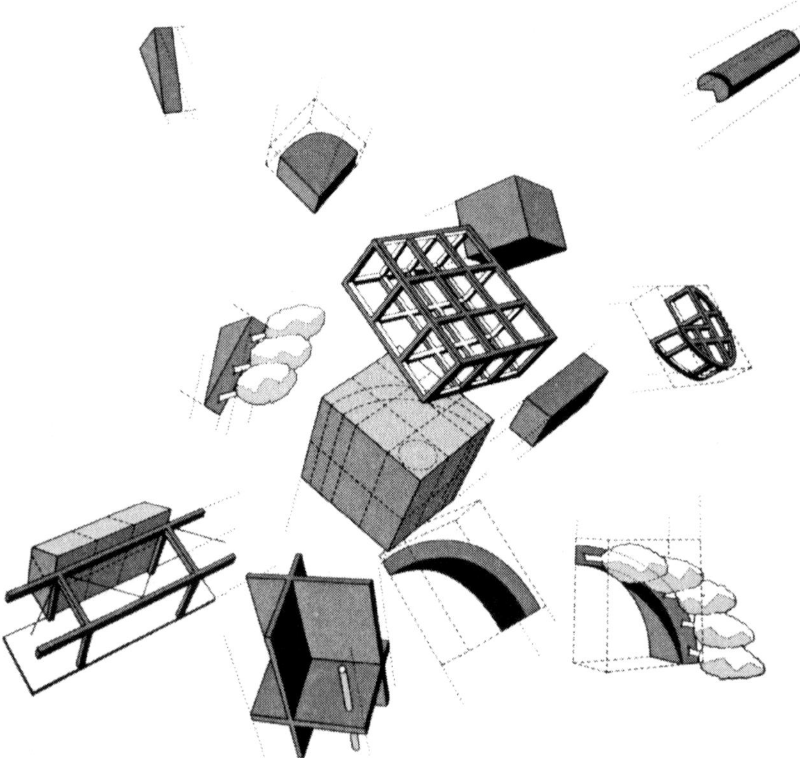

Figure 12. Exploding *Folie*. Parc de la Villette, Paris, France. Bernard Tschumi Architects.

he called it "the largest discontinuous building in the world" (Tschumi 1989, 175). The project was never intended to be the work of a single architect, for in Tschumi's design submission, the principle of dissociation extends beyond the dispersal of built mass to the author-architect himself, who works at la Villette in collaboration with a number of other architects, designers, film makers, philosophers, and poets, in resistance to the idea of a sole creator-subject, a "master-builder" in control of the work. "The paradigm of the architect passed down to us through the modern period," Tschumi says, "is that of the form-giver, the creator of hierarchical and symbolic structures character-ized, on the one hand, by their unity of parts and, on the other, by the transparency of form to meaning" (Tschumi 1998, 207). La Villette challenges this paradigm and its "belief in the unified, centered, and self-generative subject, whose own autonomy is reflected in the formal autonomy of the work" (208). The objective is transformative, I would say, not destructive.

The same applies to *les folies*, which, Tschumi notes, are not separate buildings, but "one building exploded on the site" (qtd. in Boles 1987, 94). The *folie*, the basic unit with which each collabora-tor at la Villette is given to build and/or write, is a simple, undiffer-entiated 10 x 10 x 10 meter cube, enamelled a bright red. Without formal or functional content, each cube begins as *"une case vide,"* a blank signifier that only subsequently "receives the play of signs" (Tschumi 1987, 5). This, again, is the principle of dissociation, ap-plied here to "the disjunction between an architectural signifier and the programmatic signified" (vi): each *folie* can be divided into smaller structures, or enlarged upon through rule-based combination with additional structures such as staircases, walls, or ramps—but initially it is "independent of park, program and site" (5). The bright red *folies*, regularly distributed on a grid, comprise only one system (the "system of points") of the three that make up Tschumi's tripartite, layering, design scheme for la Villette; the "system of lines" and the "system of surfaces" are as fundamental, he says, as the "system of points." Each of these layers "represents a different and autonomous system (a text), whose superimposition on another makes impossible any 'composi-tion,' maintaining differences and refusing ascendancy of any privi-leged system or organizing element" (vi). Although one could argue, Tschumi says, that "the same architect continues his controlling activity by staging the superimposition (and hence that the park remains the product of his individual intentions), the composition requirements provided a means to relativize the presence of such a masterminding subject" (vi). Another layer can always be interposed, another juxtaposition can be introduced by a different designer, so that each version of la Villette is but the receptacle of another. "Such juxtapositions would be successful only insofar as they injected discordant notes into the system, hence reinforcing a specific aspect of the Park theory. The principle of heterogeneity—of multiple, dissociated and inherently confrontational elements—is aimed at disrupting the smooth coherence and reassuring stability of composition, promoting instability and programmatic madness ('a *folie*')" (vi).

La folie, "madness," is a "constant point of reference" at the Parc de la Villette (Tschumi 1987, 16). Whereas in the discourse of modernity, *la folie* belongs on the other side of the reason/madness binary out of which, as Foucault demonstrates in *Madness and Civilization*, modern rationality emerged, at la Villette, the relationship between "reason" and "madness," "normality" and "deviation" is "not a coupling of opposites" (27). The *folies*, for instance, can be built to meet programmatic needs *only as deviations* from the norm, and "normality" is "only one possibility among those offered by the combination, the 'genetics' of architectural elements" (17). I suggest in chapter 1, following Lennard Davis, that in much the same way that the targeting of "madness" at the close of the Middle Ages facilitated the definition of a new rational self, the eighteenth century "became deaf," preoccupied with the otherness of "deafness," by way of consolidating Enlightenment ideas about subjectivity and body. The "madness" of la Villette disrupts the Enlightenment's same/different oppositions, including its phonocentric binary before/after, presence/absence, hearing/deafness—with all of the ontological and political freight that the binary bears. For this is a collaboration in which the author does not put himself first—at and as the center—and, for this reason, the system is designed *to space*: resisting hierarchy, it moves not up, but out. A "writing of space, a mode of spacing," la Villette, as Derrida describes it, "exposes itself to the outside and spaces itself out" (Pf 65). The word, *la folie*, suggests madness, lunacy, "the fool, the absentminded, the wanderer: *the one who is spacy or spaced-out*" (75); also a building, a lunatic asylum to which unreason is confined. Tschumi selected the term, he says, to free it from its negative historical connotations (Tschumi 1987, 16–17), and at the same time, to open signification to the "experience of spacing" (Pf 65). It is not insignificant, then, that *la folie* means pleasure-palace as well, and that *folie* leads back historically to *folle*, the erotic, lewd, and wanton (female) body that every architecture in the service of metaphysics has relegated to the other side of its either/or. Not the least, the bright blood-red *folies*, built on ground previously occupied by the Paris slaughterhouses, are reminders of the violence with which metaphysics, when it collapses space, crosses out the animal body.[12] And as Derrida notes in his reading of Aristotle's theory of metaphor (a point that Ricoeur, by the way, does not take up), it is by positing the difference between phonetic speech and mere "animalistic aping" (this presupposing the difference between hearing and deafness), that metaphysics erects its man/animal opposition (MP 237).[13]

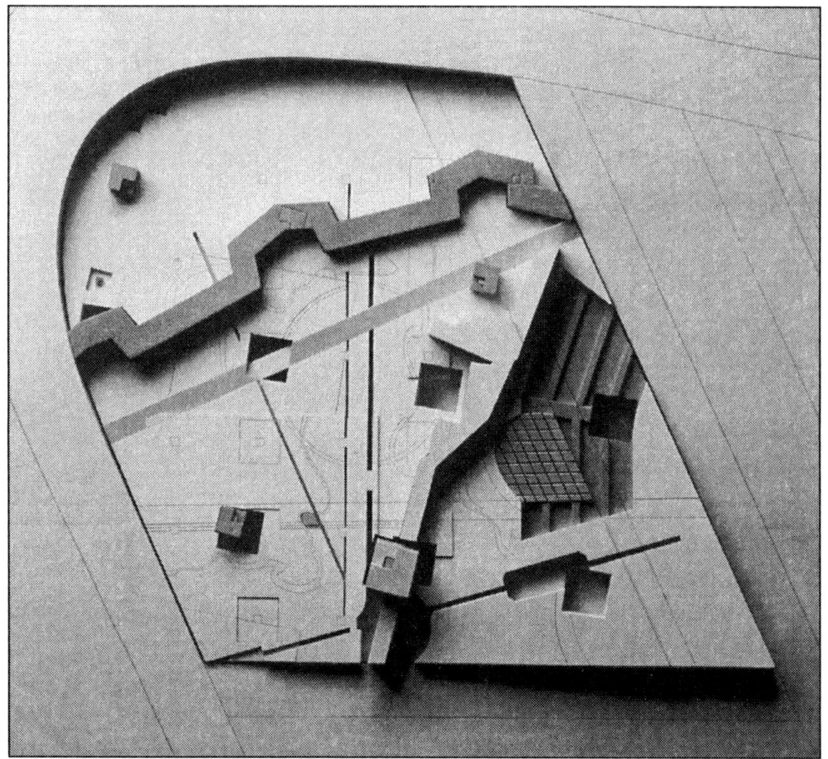

Figure 13. La Villette, Paris, France. Presentation model of second scheme for *Chora L* garden. September 1986. Eisenman Robertson Architects.

Tschumi's Parc de la Villette, in his own words, is not an idealized landscape garden, "[n]ot the *hortus conclusus* and not the replica of Nature" (Tschumi 1989, 181). The same can be said of the "garden" *folie* that was designed for la Villette by Derrida and Eisenman. Like the other *folies*, "places and spaces of *movement*" (Pf 73), the Derrida-Eisenman project is designed as a *mise-en-abyme* of layers, thus a site where movement "inscribes itself in stone" (70). In *stone*: but oscillation here is not about setting spirit free of Hegelian heavy matter, from the stone that, in Heidegger's words, "has no being at all," and *turning to stone* is not the deadly consequence of having looking at a woman's deaf and mute *os*. In the Derrida-Eisenman garden, a *folie* cast entirely in stone, sound materializes in matter, and stone becomes "the voluminous text of multiple writings," a palimpsest or grid, "mobile, light and abyssal, foliated, foliiform" (70). The *folie* has the name "*Chora*," in part because Derrida's first contribution to the project was "*Chora*," his essay on the *Timaeus*. From this essay, we can derive some of the "principles of construction" with which he and Eisenman worked in their collaboration, principles that I take to be relevant to the founding of the university as also a place and space of movement—of movement, understood not as withdrawal or as verticality, but as deferral, opening out.

In Derrida's essay, *chora*, the Platonic metaphor, has obvious architectural relevance, though not along the lines suggested by Alberto Pérez-Gómez, not as facilitating a depth hermeneutics that elevates architecture above technics; not as the ground or support of a philosophy—or an institution—of the subject. The whole history of interpretations of the *Timaeus* is characterized by such attempts to appropriate *chora* as ground, Derrida says. Layer upon layers of readings—"rich, numerous, inexhaustible, the interpretations come" (CW 17)—try "to give form to the meaning of *chora*" (17), they "buzz and hum around *chora*, taking charge of it/her by overloading it/her with inscriptions or reliefs, giving it/her form, imprinting it/her with types" (18–19), in order to determine it/her as the support of some anthropomorphic schema or some philosophy of the subject.[14] But "*chora* is not a subject" (17) in the *Timaeus*, not the subject, nor the subject's support, and precisely for this reason, it is an apt figure for the Parc de la Villette, where the paradigm of the subject is displaced. In keeping with Tschumi's purpose at la Villette, Plato's *chora* actually "provokes and resists any binary or dialectical determination, any inspection of a philosophical type" (19). In the *Timaeus*, Derrida points out, *chora* does not belong either to the *logos* or to metaphor understood as a *mythos* that stands under philosophy's watchful eye. Plato's *chora* is not a word-trope of the sort that Ricoeur dismisses, but neither is it a proper name. "We shall not speak of metaphor, but not in order to hear, for example, that the *chora* is *properly* a mother, a nurse, a receptacle, a bearer of imprints or of gold" (16). Indeed, *chora* "would trouble the very order of polarity" (16), including the polarity of proper sense and metaphorical sense; also, then, polarities of the sexual type, for *chora* is, Plato says, a *triton genus* that does not belong to either the intelligible or the sensible, not to any either/or.[15] Like the "third ear" I consider in chapter 4, this *triton genus* is a hybrid or bastard structure; it belongs to an other.[16] What distinguishes *chora*, "the natural receptacle of all bodies" (Plato 1965, 69), is that it receives and gives place to all types, is a receptacle for them, and yet "never itself takes a permanent impress from any of the things that enter it" (69). A kind of *tympan* that both precedes and exceeds what is inscribed, *chora*, the print-bearer, as Plato calls it, would be the place-space that is always ready to receive another imprint without ever becoming what it receives, "the neutral space of a place without place, a place where everything is marked but which would be 'in itself' unmarked" (CW 23). Site of a *mise-en-abyme* that "gives place" to every discourse without belonging to it, *chora* is about "the structure of an overprinting without a base" (21).

It is significant that Plato compares *chora* to a winnowing basket that is shaken to sort and clean corn, for there is movement—not up but out—involved in its abysssal overprinting, in *chora*'s status as a sieve that sifts layer after layer of interpretations. A receptacle of receptacles, "*chora* shakes, shakes the whole, separating before the separation," Jeffrey Kipnis remarks (in terms that recall Heidegger's *Geschlechtlosigkeit*); "it is a movement before movement begins, since in the *Timaeus* all true movement begins with the world-soul and comes after the Demiurge does his work. Yet *chora* shakes and orders even the chaos. Thus *chora solicits* in the Derridean sense of the term" (Kipnis 1989, 149).[17] This shaking-solicitation has to do with the "structural law" that, Derrida says, the *Timaeus*, by way of *chora*, describes, which is also the structure that Plato's text inscribes. Drawing out this analogy between description and inscription in the *Timaeus*, "Derrida develops a new strategy for reading (Plato), one which finds evidence of *chora* already at work in Plato's text," Kipnis suggests. "In brief, he combs out formal analogies between the textural structures of the *Timaeus* and what is said of *chora* in that text" (148). We should add that this method of "combing" reinscribes the spacing movement of Plato's *chora* in Derrida's essay "*Chora*," which then becomes structurally analogous to the *Timaeus*, another instance of the shaking movement being read—as if one text were the receptacle of another; as if to describe Plato's *chora* were to inscribe the back-and-forth rhythm of winnowing. For instance, what Plato's text says about *chora* as a receptacle that opens to all things but that cannot "itself" be apprehended, Derrida finds to be demonstrated by the *Timaeus*, where, to recall the origin of the Athenians, it is necessary to move back through oral tale-tellings to a moment before their own memory and to an archaic, pre-originary, writing, "the graphic vestiges of *another place*" (CW 25). It is necessary to go back to an origin that precedes philosophy where, however, memory is already inscribed, "as if painted with indelible letters," as Derrida cites Plato (26).[18] In Plato's text, "[e]ach tale is thus the *receptacle of another*" (26), so that writing-reading becomes a constant movement of going outside of itself. Plato's text, and Derrida's in turn, stages this movement of going out and going back through a series of unfolding displacements: "The whole of the *Timaeus* [and of Derrida's "*Chora*"] thus scans to the rhythm of steps backwards" (30)—which is not, however, withdrawal or gathering since no halting ground is ever reached, no boundary that forces the steps to stop. Movement without limit: "We no longer know whence comes at times the feeling of dizziness, on what edges, against the inside face of what wall: chaos, chasms, *ch-o-ra*" (24).

In the *Timaeus*, Derrida notes, *chora*, this "non-Platonic" element intrinsic to the Platonic text, appears for the first time right in the middle of the book, at the most interior place, but as an irreducible exteriority that philosophy cannot assimilate. Interestingly for my topic in this book, Derrida refers to *chora*, this figure (folding) of the outside inside, this "open chasm in the middle of the book," as a "gaping mouth" (CW 21). In the Derrida-Eisenman garden at the Parc de la Villette, the open mouth is cast in stone, but not as the deaf-mute *os* of a Medusa, not as a *monstrum* that petrifies a spectating male. Planted at a "dizzy tilt" in their unnatural garden (a garden designed to admit of no vegetation, and to be made entirely of water and stone), the Derrida-Eisenman *chora* looks something like a tympanum. On the insistence of Eisenman, who wanted their collaboration "to be more than the simple aggregation of two soloists, a writer and an architect" (98), Derrida initiated the design of the *chora* sculpture with a sketch: "On returning from New York, in the airplane, I wrote Eisenman a letter containing a drawing and its interpretation" (98). Derrida's drawing, his "approximate 'representation'" or "'materialization'" (98) of the Platonic figure, was the sketch of a lyre and/ or a sieve. The sieve (grill or grid) recalls "the way in which the place (the *chora*) filters the 'types,' the forces or seeds that have been impressed on it," while the lyre (a word that is homographic in French and English and also close to layer) suggests a musical event, "a stringed musical instrument (piano, harp, lyre?: strings, stringed instrument, vocal chords, etc.)" (98). Derrida wanted the sculpture, cast in gold, to be planted obliquely in the earth. He suggested that nothing should be inscribed on it, save perhaps a signature, and "one or two Greek words (*plokanon, seiomena,* etc.)" (99).

Working from Derrida's essay on the *Timaeus* as well as from some preliminary designs for the work, Eisenman came up with a title for the collaborative garden: he called the project not just *Chora* but *Chora L Work*. With the addition of the final L, the name *chora* is carried over into song, Derrida suggests: "With the final *L, chora L: chora* becomes more liquid or more aerial, I do not dare to say, more feminine" (CW 97). The title, like Derrida's sketch, suggests at once a musical instrument, vocal chords, and a concert of voices, "the multiple chorale, the *chora* of *Chora L Work*" (98). Thus, in Derrida's words, "this title is more than a title. It also draws a signature and the mark of a plural signature, written by both of us in concert" (97). The garden *folie*, like the other accompanying performances at the Parc de la Villette, "becomes musical, an architecture for many voices, at once different and harmonized in their very alterity" (97). On this matter of an architecture for many voices, I should say again that the Derrida-Eisenman garden is designed as but one receptacle within the larger layered receptacle (of receptacles) of the Parc de la Villette, a site Tschumi designed on the layering principle of superimposition. And on the matter of receptacles, I should mention as well that the final *L* in the title *Chora L Work* recalls, as does the empty cube, the red *folie*, the "el," the three-sided portion of a hollow cube that Eisenman has used in designing several houses. House X, for example, is the result of "the manipulation of four of these "els" separated by a cruciform void at the heart of the house." This project attempts "to suspend the human subject—whether creator or spectator," Jean-François Bédard notes (Bédard 1994, 11). To extend the process of layering: "House IIa, like the two other houses of that period, was assembled (or rather, decomposed) from House X's els" (12). Additional layers could be sifted through: for example, Eisenman discovered surprising relationships between the site of la Villette, including its 1867 abattoir, and the project that he designed in 1978 for the Cannaregio quarter of Venice, a project that layers the grid for Le Corbusier's hospital with a building derived from House IIa (see Eisenman 1994, 186–196; CW 69–72; 92). This sieving of sites and layers would have to include the point-grid layering structure itself, one that Tschumi uses at la Villette, that Eisenman used at Cannaregio in 1978 and, moving back, that Tschumi used in 1977 in Joyce's Garden, which is based in turn on *Finnegan's Wake* (see CW 82–83).

Not the least, where lyres and layers are concerned, note should be made of the discovery that the shape of the site for the *Chora L Work* garden was very close to the shape of Derrida's drawing of the sieve-lyre (CW 92). So, Derrida asks, what does Eisenman do with that? "He translates, transposes, transforms and appropriates my letter, rewriting it in *his* languages, in his *languages*, both architectural and others. He brings another form to the developing architectural structure (a structure that is already quite fixed): that of a lyre, lying down at an oblique angle. Then, in a change of scale, he reinscribes it in its very interior, as a small lyre within a large one" (99). A lyre within a lyre: "'Lyre,' 'layers,' would thus be a good title, overtitle, or sub-title for *Chora L Work*" (99). The title "says the truth [of the work] in a word which is many words, a kind of many leafed book, but that is also the visible figure of the lyre, the visibility of an instrument which foments the invisible: music" (99). The truth of *Chora L Work*, the truth that the lyre or layer says, is not the truth of subjective self-presence. "It gives rise to no revelation of presence, still less to an adequation. It is an irreducible inadequation which we have just evoked; and also a challenge to the subjectile" (99).

SIGNATURES

So, the *chora* is space, spacing.

—Derrida, "Transcript Seven" of *Chora L Works*

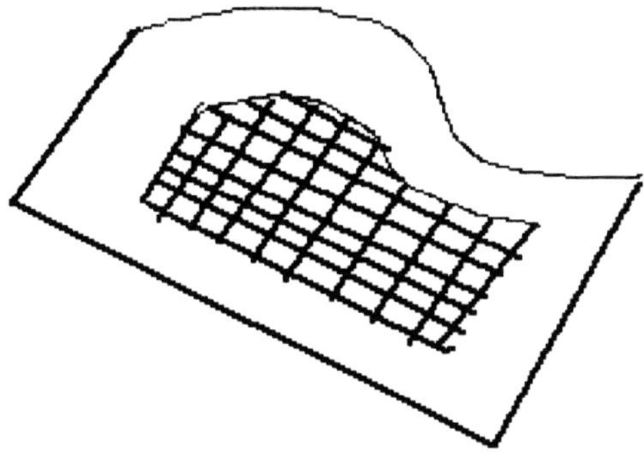

This is my rough computer-drawn replication of Derrida's "approximate 'representation' " of *chora* as both a lyre and a sieve. In closing, I add, superpose, it as a supplement, a surplus- or sub-signature layered onto this chorale work. Because, as a sieve, *chora* oscillates before linear order is imposed, and because it is imprinted prior to phonetic speech, it shakes up the philosopher's, and the university's, supposed grounding in *hearing-oneself-speak.*

As a lyre, the figure also evokes for me the myth of the Sirens. Like the Sphinx, the Sirens were hybrid creatures, usually represented as birds with women's heads, and shown singing and playing their flutes and lyres. It is said that their beautiful, if melancholy, voices posed grave danger, even the threat of death, to men who passed by their island, and so for this reason, as a defense, it was necessary to cut their tongues off from male ears. As in the case of Medusa, the Sirens, whose "power depends emphatically on hearing" (Segal 1994b, 100), are thus muted when Odysseus, ordering himself strapped to the mast, stops the ears of his fellow sailors with wax.

Here, again, is a kind of Medusa effect: the male ear is effectively severed, his hearing cut off, in this fantastic story about the deadly danger of the female voice, the feared *os(sis)* I have been writing about in this book. I like to think that the *Chora L* lyre unsettles this founding fantasy, so as to allow for—so as to attune the university to—multiple ways to hear.

NOTES

CHAPTER ONE. MOURNING THE VOICE

1. The modern viewing subject, along with its constitutive signifying process, is, to use Julia Kristeva's words from "Holbein's Dead Christ" (in *Black Sun*), "isolated, pruned, condensed, reduced" (Kristeva 1989, 115). It will be my task in this book to argue that the isolation and reduction have to do particularly with the viewing subject's ear.

2. I concur with Mieke Bal in *Double Exposures* on the point that it is impossible to define vision, including modern vision, in unified and essentialist terms, as the ocularcentric narrative does; there are, she suggests, "differentiating modes, if not kinds of vision," and our practices of reading should accordingly endeavor to proliferate points of view (Bal 1996, 9). Like Bal, my strategy will be to multiply perspectives—on ways of hearing, however, and not just looking.

3. In the Western philosophical tradition, the voice, says Rée, is at one with "'spirituality', 'identity,' 'conscience,' 'mentality,' 'interiority,' or 'subjectivity'" (Rée 1999, 2–3).

4. See Martin Jay's comprehensive analysis in *Downcast Eyes* of the shift that takes place with Descartes to "modern ocularcentrism." As should be evident by now, I take issue with Jay's thesis that modernity is based solely on the eye; as will become evident in later pages, I also take issue with his contention that "postmodern" French writing, particularly Derrida's, is an "essentially ocularphobic discourse" (15).

5. While it is not an examination of the phonocentric ear or of the role of hearing in Derrida's work, Robert Smith's incisive study *Derrida and Autobiography* is an important resource for my work in this book. I am also indebted to Gregory Ulmer's "Sounding the Unconscious," and I draw much from Derrida's *The Ear of the Other*.

6. Sacks alludes to this spatialization when he remarks that much of what seems to occur linearily in speech is "multileveled" in sign language, so that "what looks so simple is extraordinarily complex and consists of innumerable spatial patterns nested, three-dimensionally, in each other" (Sacks 1989, 87). By the same token, lip reading, "an extremely inadequate word for the complex art of observation, inference, and inspired guess-work which goes on" (2), entails spacing, the gap or

delay between what is spoken and what the lip reader pieces together to hear. Whether it proceeds by the reading of hands, lips, or written words, or by the movement of sound waves imprinting the body, deaf hearing, because it is so radically embodied, breaches the space-time closure of metaphysics, "temporal presence as point [*stigmè*] of the moment [*nun*]" (OG 12).

7. As a partial exception to this omission, see Enterline's (2000, 45) discussion of Echo and Narcissus. The exception does not really alter my point, however, which is that Enterline's study of the voice and vocal trauma, as fine as it is, all but leaves out the ear.

8. For reasons that will continue to emerge in this chapter, I cannot adopt Enterline's term "phonographic" to describe the imaginary that is at issue in the present book. I take her point in *The Rhetoric of the Body* (2000, 12) that no sooner is a phonocentric fantasy entertained than it is eroded, since subjects, and not only Ovidian subjects, are embodied and thus necessarily caught up in the "graphing" of signifiers. Nevertheless, the *fantasy* that concerns me has it otherwise: according to the fantasy of the lost voice/ear, the original *phoné* is precisely what precedes, and thus escapes, the graphic.

9. As C. D. O'Malley notes, it was Gabriello Fallopio (c.1523–62) who, in his *Observationes anatomicae*, first called attention to the third ossicle of the ear overlooked by Vesalius, who had described only the malleus and the incus. Despite his description of the third ossicle, Fallopio attributed its discovery to Ingrassia. As for Vesalius, he had already heard of the third ossicle, and had sought and found it himself, before reading Fallopio's *Observationes*. This must have been between 1555 and 1559, O'Malley suggests, "as the revised edition of the *Fabrica* makes no mention of the ossicle" (291). It may be that Vesalius became "acquainted with the third ossicle from the reference to it—an unacknowledged borrowing from Ingrassia—by Valverde in 1556. In the *Examen*, his reply to Fallopio's *Observationes*, Vesalius tells how,

> When I was cleaning a skull for preparation of a skeleton, an ossicle chanced to fall out of the ear; I opened the auditory organ in a fresh skull, and with that ossicle I found a second. I have described the incident [in the *Fabrica*] exactly as it occurred. Later I heard that a third ossicle had also been discovered, and I soon found that one that is so slight that I felt compelled to praise the carefulness of Ingrassia, the distinguished Sicilian physician who had observed it. I was happy, too, to accept its comparison with the stirrup. (O'Malley, 291)

10. Jonathan Sawday in "The Fate of Marsyas: Dissecting the Renaissance Body" points out that in the frontispiece to Vesalius's 1543 *De Humani Corporis Fabrica*, a page that demonstrates all that is "new" in the new anatomy of Vesalius, the body being dissected is certainly a female corpse; rather than prone, as was previously the situation of the body in such representations, the corpse has been elevated slightly and rotated ninety degrees, so that the gaze of the spectators is directed from the feet up to the genital organs. See also Sawday's *The Body Emblazoned* (1995). No less than Dürer's woodcut, *Draughtsman Drawing a Nude*, Vesalius's frontispiece suggests that modernity is a new way of looking. But let's remember that Fallopio, who discovered and named the female egg tubes, was first and foremost an anatomist of the ear.

11. See "Canons and Metonymies," 207–208, for Derrida's comments on the "Kantian elements" that are present in Heidegger's discourse on the university, in particular in his Rectorate Address. This is a point I return to in chapter 2, where the issue of academic freedom, always important to my discussion in this book, is considered more fully than it is in chapter 1.

12. See Derrida's comments in *Of Spirit*, Chapters VI and VII, as to the privilege Heidegger accords to the German language in his *Introduction to Metaphysics*. The link between national language and spirit, and between this and animality, is crucial to Derrida's assessment of phonocentrism as the means through which the "political" most fully operates.

CHAPTER TWO. THE ARCHITECTURE OF INSTITUTION

1. I am following the translation of Derrida's Columbia lecture by Richard Rand and Amy Wygant that is published in this Alabama collection, *Logomachia: The Conflict of the Faculties*. Derrida's lecture was first published as "Mochlos; ou, le conflit des facultés" in *Philosophie* 2 (April 1984): 21–53.

2. *Mochlos*, then, provides a point of departure, a place from which I begin in this book to reexamine the modern concept of the university. Derrida's title word, *mochlos*, also suggests a heading, a headland, a *cap* ("A title is always a heading [*cap*]" [OH 13]), a point of land that juts out into the sea, a promontory from which to head off toward another kind of university grounding. It "could be a wooden beam" with which one pushes off, "a lever for displacing a boat, a wedge for opening or closing a door, something, in short, to lean on for forcing and displacing" (M 31). *Mochlos* could be the Kantian university foundation itself, the foundational text, *The Conflict*, from which and with which Derrida pushes off in his Columbia essay to another university heading. Derrida returns to *The Conflict of the Faculties* and to the issues Kant's text raises—including the inside/outside boundary, the constative/performative distinction, and the question of university freedom—at a 1999 New Zealand conference on the university, the papers from which are published in Laurence Simmons and Heather Worth, eds., *Derrida Downunder* (2001), a collection that contains Derrida's "The Future of the Profession or the Unconditional University," and "A Roundtable Discussion With Jacques Derrida." A slightly different version of "The Future of the Profession" is published in *Without Alibi* (2002) as "The University Without Condition."

3. Derrida comments in "Canons and Metonymies" on yet another reason for the choice of the title word *mochlos*: "deprived of an article and placed in a title, it resembles a proper name. And in this resemblance to 'someone,' it seemed to me as monstrous, gigantic and dangerous as a mean animal, a dog for example (in French a *molosse* is a big watch dog whose name comes from the Greek *molossos*, a dog from the land of *Molossia*; or that big Australian lizard, the 'Moloch,' an animal more than twenty centimeters long covered with spines; or that giant and mythical serpent called the Loch Ness monster. A fantastic expandable serpent: It resembles a *phallos*, doesn't it? The proper name of a giant and slightly monstrous, inhuman animal: This is what I understand in the hollow or the hole (*Loch*) or the lack (*los*, loss) of this name, *Mochlos*" (CM 204).

4. The German title of Kant's polemic is *Von einem neuerdings erhobenen vornehmen Ton in der Philosophie* (in *Schriften zur Metaphysik und Logik, Volume III* [Wiesbaden: Insel-Verlag, 1958], 377–97). The French translation by L. Guillermit gives the title as *D'un ton grand seigneur adopté naguère en philosophie* (in *Première introduction à la critique de la faculté de juger* [Paris: Vrin, 1975], 86–109). The title of Derrida's 1982 essay on Kant's polemic is translated by John Leavey as "Of an Apocalyptic Tone Recently Adopted in Philosophy" (in *Semeia* 23: 63–97). Leavey translates Kant's title as "Of an Overlordly Tone Recently Adopted in Philosophy." More recently, in *Raising the Tone of Philosophy: Late Essays by Immanuel Kant, Transformative Critique by Jacques Derrida* (1993), Peter Fenves translates Kant's title as "On A Newly Arisen Superior Tone in Philosophy." Fenves translates Derrida's 1982 essay as "On a Newly Arisen Apocalyptic Tone in Philosophy." I include a chapter-length reading of Derrida's reading in "Of an Apocalyptic Tone," of Kant's "Of an Overlordly Tone" in my book *Posts* (Albany: State University of New York Press, 1996).

5. For Derrida's full analysis of the constative/performative distinction, see his *Limited INC* (1977).

6. There is, it seems to me, an obvious coding of sexual difference in Kant's *ergon/parergon* distinction in *The Conflict*. Derrida deals with this coding, particularly in Kant's *Critique of Judgement*, in the first essay of *The Truth in Painting*.

7. In a system of pure philosophy, the philosopher, the metaphysician, "will have to operate like a good architect, *like* a good *tekhnites* of edification," Derrida writes in *The Truth in Painting*. " He will be a sort of artist. Now what does a good architect do, according to Kant? He must first of all be certain of the ground, the foundation, the fundament" (TP 40).

8. The university stands upright, "rises" to its idea, as John Henry Newman put it, only if it remains faithful to its founding and foremost principle, "knowledge as its own end." Without this principle of reason, the university degenerates into a technical school, "a sort of bazaar, or pantechnicon" in which, Newman says, "wares of all kinds are heaped together for sale in stalls independent of each other" (qtd. in Pelikan 1992, 57). Jaroslav Pelikan's book is one of several recent attempts to recover Newman's (and Kant's) idea of a university. Among these studies, a consensus exists on this point: the university is not "a trade school that prepares students to fight it out in the business jungle," as Bercuson, Bothwell, and Granastein put it in the Canadian study, *The Great Brain Robbery* (1984, 103). Theirs is a current version of the Kantian argument that, within the academy, "some areas of knowledge are more important than others" (77) and "[s]ome are better teachers than others, some do more and better research and scholarship than others; some are more valuable . . . than others" (48). I am, as is Derrida, very critical of the hirerachical difference this argument puts in place between the humanities and those fields that are caught up with technics—as if the humanities were not implicated in technics themselves. There is, I contend, no "place" outside of technology from which to launch a critique of technology, an argument that Derrida makes in his reading of Heidegger's *The Question Concerning Technology*. Moreover, the assumption by the humanities of such a (Kantian) non-technological place has contributed, more than anything else, to their "irrelevance," and thus their demise, in the modern university. This argument has everything to do with the idealizing notion that "speech" is untainted by technology and that "hearing" of speech is similarly unmediated by any "typographics."

9. In "The Principle of Reason: The University in the Eyes of its Pupils," Derrida draws out the assumption of the Aristotelian model, because: "Kant, Nietzsche and Heidegger, speaking of the university, premodern or modern, do not say exactly what Aristotle said, nor do all three of them say exactly the same thing. But they *also* do say the same thing" (PR, 18). For Aristotle, Derrida says, the philosopher, who is an architect and a leader, is also "in essence a *teacher*. Beyond the fact of knowing causes and of possessing reason [*to logon ekhein*], he bears another mark [*semeion*] of recognition: the 'capacity to teach' [*to dunasthai didaskein*]. To teach, then, and at the same time to direct, steer, organize the empirical work of the laborers. The theoretician-teacher or 'architect' is a leader because he is on the side of the *arkhe*, of beginning and commanding. He commands—he is the premier or the prince—because he knows causes and principles, the 'whys' and thus also the 'wherefores' of things. Before the fact, and before anyone else, he answers to the principle of reason which is the first principle, the principle of principles. And that is why he takes orders from no one; it is he, on the contrary, who orders, prescribes, lays down the law" (PR 18).

10. The lower faculty, while farthest away from the exercise of power, would be closest to the ear of the state. This as another example of how Kant takes in what he excludes. His remark illustrates the way in which, as Derrida says in "Tympan," two kinds of appropriating mastery, hierarchy and envelopment, communicate with each other: "they both follow the movement of the same wheel, whether it is a question, finally, of Heidegger's hermeneutical circle or of Hegel's ontological circle" (MP xx). Both follow the spiraling border of *The Conflict of the Faculties*, where the interiorizing and hierarchizing of philosophy within the university is also an *envelopment*—of the higher faculties by the lower faculty, of political power by pure reason. It seems that each time an oppositional, hierarchical boundary is declared, another exteriority is enveloped, or consumed; and this, paradoxically, in the name of animating the university body and of balancing its left and right sides.

CHAPTER THREE. PASSAGES

1. Less implacable, perhaps, than the Sphinx are the huge Memnon statues such at those at Thebes; "grandiose and massive," as Hegel describes them, hewn from a single stone, these immense figures can be partly human in form, indicating that, already in Egypt, spirit is on the way to fashioning a shape adequate to itself. The Memnons are transitional, moreover, because when light strikes them at dawn, they utter (however minimal) a sound; slight reverberations arise and then vanish again. Since stones do not "sound spontaneously as organic bodies do, but only when they are struck" (Hegel 1970, 138), since, to emit sound, they must receive their light from without, the Memnons are "more inorganic and architectural than sculptural" constructions (Hegel 1975 II, 643); arranged in rows, "resting in themselves, motionless, the arms glued to the body, the feet firmly fixed together, numb, stiff, and lifeless, [they] are set up facing the sun in order to await its ray to touch them and give them soul and sound" (Hegel 1975 I, 358).

2. Derrida writes in *The Gift of Death* that the narrative of history as a *passage* to freedom and responsibility involves the notion of delivery from the *daimonic*, the

mystagogic, the enthusiastic and the esoteric (GD 3). Such a narrative comprises "a genealogy of the subject who says 'myself,' the subject's relation to itself as an instance of liberty, singularity and responsibility, the relation to self as being before the other" (3). The self who puts itself first is the anchor of every phono(audio)centric system.

3. Derrida does not translate the word *Sittlichkeit*, which, however, means something like ethical life; the moment where spirit externalizes itself in the laws and institutions of "the existing [*vorhandenen*] world" (Hegel 1991, 189).

4. See Kelly Oliver (1997, 37–38) on the figure of the woman and the principle of the feminine in Hegel's dialectic.

5. For Hegel, only speculative philosophy should be taught in the university, and only subjects that are preparatory to speculative philosophy should be included in a pre-university (*Gymnasium*) curriculum. See Derrida's discussion in "The Age of Hegel" of the way that Hegel's argument to this effect is itself "familial" in structure, an instance of the circle of return to the (name of the) father: in the university, no teaching except Hegel's can, Hegel says, claim the name of philosophy proper. Hegel's argument is "familial" in another sense as well: it is presented under the guise of an autobiographical confiding, with the circular *"already-not-yet"* ("The Age of Hegel," 4) structure that, for Hegel, autobiography entails. Hegel's argument, found in "To the Royal Ministry of Spiritual, Academic, and Medical Affairs" (1822), is appended to Derrida's essay, "The Age of Hegel." This essay is reprinted in *Who's Afraid of Philosophy: Right to Philosophy I* (2002, 117–57).

6. "Homogeneous, concentric, and circulating indefinitely, the movement of the whole is remarked in the partial determinations of the system" (MP xx).

7. The woman anoints, shrouds, mourns, and monumentalizes the man's corpse, "prevents the corpse from returning to nature. In embalming it, in shrouding it, in enclosing it in bands of material, of language, and of writing, in putting up the stele, this operation raises the corpse to the universality of spirit" (G 144a).

8. While "Hegel's feminine is *in its principle* unconscious and inarticulate," Kelly Oliver notes (Oliver 1997, 38), "philosophy is the activity of articulating the concept of consciousness, or articulating what we mean by consciousness. To put it simply, the goal of philosophy is to articulate fully the meaning of consciousness such that there is no difference between that meaning and its articulation. If this goal is reached, nothing remains unconscious or unspoken" (35). Nothing remains, not least the woman—figure of the inarticulate, of the unconscious; figure of remains.

9. A crucial text here, and basic to my study overall, is Derrida's interview, "'Eating Well,' or the Calculation of the Subject," particularly as concerns the "passage through the mouth" in metaphysics.

10. For Hegel, color marks a step in the elevation, the uplifting, of sensuous matter, just as particular colors themselves symbolize some placement on the ascending scale. Blue, he says, is lower than red. Blue is the color of the woman, of the mother; and as such, is passive, "milder, sensuous, more tranquil" than the active "masculine, dominant red" (Hegel 1975 II, 841–42). Blue is the color of the woman who is nearer than man to the plant, nearer to the half-light or the half-life ("the Hegelian system commands that it be read as a book of life" [G 83a]), somewhere between nature and spirit. Unlike Hegel, who adopts Goethe's theory of color, Julia

Kristeva in *Desire In Language*, commenting on Giotto's Padua frescoes, chooses to read blue as a peripheral, and thus radical, color that "takes hold of the viewer at the extreme limit of visual perception" (Kristeva 1980, 224). It is blue in particular that, she says, has the potential to decenter the specular subject at the fetishizing moment and to lessen "both object identification and phenomenal fixation" (225).

11. According to Freud, a son placed as Derrida is in *Glas* between a father and a mother, can only be fraught with castration anxiety, and must needs create the fetish as a defense against the loss that he fears. The fetish acts as a disavowal of, and substitute for, the mother's perceived-to-be missing member, her cut-off body part. It stands in for the thing that the son knows his father to have and sees his mother to be missing, the thing that the son does not want to give up. We might say then, that in the act of turning his name into a thing, Derrida fetishizes his signature in *Glas*. Staging the male's (son's) fear of having his phallic privilege removed, Derrida translates Freud's account of fetishism "into a fetishistic writing" (Todd 1990, 108). Spivak suggests as much when she reads Derrida's signature, his d-words scattered between the two columns (legs) of *Glas*, "as a discharge of dissemination into the (n)ever-ravished fold of the hymen" (Spivak 1977, 26). However, see also note 15 below, as to how my reading here differs from Spivak's.

12. "Production, differentiation, opposition are bound to the value of activity. That is the system of virility" (G 113a) that the Hegelian system is.

13. Like the book, *Glas*, and the fetishism it stages, this woman is a "monster," source of both fascination and dread. I am thinking here, particularly in view of the "structural similarity" of vagina and ear, of Laura Mulvey's reference, in *Fetishism and Curiosity*, to the way Barabara Creed traces the "monstrous feminine" in horror movies to the figure of the mother in Kristeva's psychoanalytic theory of the abject. As Mulvey quotes Creed on this archaic mother: "Within patriarchal signifying practices, particularly the horror film, she is reconstructed and represented as a negative figure, one associated with the dread of the generative mother seen only in the abyss, the monstrous vagina, the origin of all life threatening to absorb what it once birthed. . . . In horror films such as *Alien*, we are given a representation of the female genitals as uncanny, horrific objects of dread and fascination" (Mulvey 1996, 63–64). Mary Russo might call the hymen-tympan between the columns of *Glas* the "space of the female grotesque." Such space leaves room for chance, and for the mistakes— "noise, dissonance, or monstrosity"—that are not allowed "within the very constrained spaces of normalization" (Russo 1994, 10–11).

14. Hegel's *Letters*, from which Derrida quotes at length in *Glas*, would themselves be absolutely unassimilable to Hegel's philosophical system. Certainly, through Christiane alone, they contaminate Hegel's family schema; and through the bastard son Ludwig, they give the lie to Hegel's claim that the end is already there at the start, that the germ of his family system was already intact in Jena.

15. In Hegel, Geoffrey Hartman points out, "relations of *voix* and *voie*, of father and son, of foundation and filiation" (1975, 765), come together. One thing that interests me in Derrida's countersignature, as taking on the cadence of a woman's voice, is the alternate *voie*, movement, it gives to writing. I do not read Derrida's signature in *Glas* as modeled on masturbation, the business Spivak suggests of ejaculating, discharging, the signature as semen. And unlike Hartman, I do not read the

rhythm of *Glas* as, simply, a movement of getting it up and letting it fall, where just "as the phallic statue is being erected in one column, the signature falls in the other" (Hartman 1975, 776). I consider the countersignature, the d-stroke in *Glas*, as more akin to sound waves that move laterally, back and forth between the columns.

CHAPTER FOUR. WHO HAS EARS TO HEAR?

1. Since the publication of *Of Spirit*, there has been a significant critical discussion of spirit in Heidegger and in Derrida's reading of Heidegger's work. See for example David Wood, ed., *Of Derrida, Heidegger and Spirit*; Krell's *Daimon Life*, and his essay "Of Spirit and the *Daimon*: On Derrida's *De l'esprit*" in Dallery, Scott and Holley Roberts, *Ethics and Danger*.

2. I am thinking here not only of the title, "Living On: Borderlines," but also of what Derrida says in this essay says about surplus and survival.

3. There are, it seems to me, marked similarities between Derrida's reading of Heidegger's *Geschlechtlosigkeit* and, as should emerge in chapter 6, his reading of Plato's *chora*.

4. See Miguel de Beistegui's *Heidegger & the Political* for a careful critical discussion of Heidegger's philosophy of university, including his resistance to the university's technologization.

5. Heidegger's single blow is delivered heavy-handedly. What we hear in this single blow (in Heidegger's underlining of the word *one*, twice in a short paragraph) is the commanding voice of the Rector himself, asserting the value of mission ("the inflexibility of an order, the rigor or even the *directive* rigidity of a mission" [OS 32]), the spiritual-historical mission of the German people, and—now celebrating *Geschlecht* and *Geist* together, now underlining *geistig*—self-affirming the will to essence of the German university.

6. "Heidegger will have kept silence. He will not have spoken a single word against the event that is for ever associated with Nazi barbarity," writes Miguel de Beistegui (1998, 146). Just how to interpret Heidegger's silence, whether to think the silence as a response, what implications the silence has for our reading of Heidegger's work overall: debate on these and other related questions has led to an enormous literature on interpretation and on Heidegger interpretation in particular, a literature to which I hope this book contributes. Derrida adds significantly to this literature through his reading of Heidegger; indeed, the literature includes many critical readings of Derrida and critical readings of his readings of Heidegger. Derrida and Derrida studies aside, the following are but a few of those who have contributed (for good or for ill) to this debate: Farías (1987); Lacoue-Labarthe (1990); Lang (1996); Lyotard (1990); Rockmore (1992); Spanos (1993); Wolin (1990 and 1993); Zimmerman (1990).

7. For Derrida in *Cinders*, Ned Lukacher suggests, language, like sound, is first the escape of heat. "*Il y a là cendre* initially presents itself to Derrida as a ringing tonality before it becomes a meaningful utterance. The ideal materiality of its broken music precedes the unfolding of its poetic and philosophic resonance" (Lukacher 1991, 3). The point is of course central to my thesis in this book.

8. Anne Dufourmantelle, in *Of Hospitality*, writes as follows of Derrida's "poetic hospitality" to the specter: "To the pacified reason of Kant, Derrida opposes the primary haunting of a subject prevented by alterity from closing itself off in peacefulness" (OHS 4).

9. From *Of Grammatology*: "It is thus that, after evoking the "voice of being," Heidegger recalls that it is silent, mute, insonorous, wordless, originarily *a-phonic* (*die Gewähr der lautlosen Stimme verborgener Quellen* . . .). The voice of the sources is not heard. A rupture between the originary meaning of being and the word, between meaning and the voice, between "the voice of being" and the "*phonè*," between "the call of being" and articulated sound" (OG 22).

10. I am following Derrida here in translating *die Hand* in the singular in the last sentence of the passage I am quoting, although the J. Glenn Gray translation of *Was heisst Denken?*, the translation that I am using and that is cited in John Leavey's translation of "*Geschlecht* II" (194, n12), renders the word in the plural.

CHAPTER FIVE. FOUR WAYS OF READING TWO PAIRS: OF SHOES

1. According to Hugh Silverman (1994), Derrida's essay has at least three titles. The essay was first published in *Macula* (no. 3) as "*La Verité en pointure*," which can be rendered in English as "Truth in Shoe Size." The essay was then published in Derrida's 1978 book, *La Verité en peinture* (translated 1987, *The Truth in Painting*) as the fourth essay, "*Restitutions de la verité en pointure*." An English translation of the first part of the essay also appeared in *Research in Phenomenology* in 1978 as "Restitutions." See Silverman, "The Autobiographical Textuality of Heidegger's Shoes" (1994).

2. For Jameson, Dan Latimer writes, "Van Gogh's work is the segment of an enormous circle, a hint of some vaster reality which allows us to reconstruct the whole; or to use a different figure, *inside* the work of art are, in proportion, all the elements of an *outside*. This is the depth model of interpretation, and Jameson identifies in Modernism at least four versions of it: the dialectical model of essential and apparent, the Freudian model of latent and manifest, the existential model of authentic and inauthentic, the semiotic model of signifier and signified. These disappear with the end of Modernism" (Latimer 1984, 118–19).

3. This truth-speaking subject, it seems to me, is gendered masculine, regardless of the content, or question, of the painting itself. Regardless of whether the painted shoes are worn by a woman, for instance, the viewing subject, like the Dürer draughtsman, is "naturally" male.

4. For Freud, Derrida points out, the concept of repression is "linked with the upright position, that is, to a certain *elevation*. The passage to the upright position raises man, thus distancing his nose from the sexual zones, anal or genital. This distance enobles his height and leaves its traces by delaying his action. Delay, difference, enobling elevation, diversion of the olfactory sense from the sexual stench, repression—here are the origins of morality" (Derrida, "Before the Law," 193).

5. Jameson's acute anxiety about textual and artistic practices that differ from his own recalls Freud's account of fetishism and its basis in the fear of (sexual)

difference: "The fetish allows its creator/spectator to retain a belief that antidotes an unwelcome perception, threatening to his narcissistic sense of self as whole and immortal, for if the feminine body can be 'castrated,' thus the logic, his own penis is in danger; if the other body can die, his own survival is at stake" (Bronfen 1992, 97).

6. The (Kantian) question, again, of finding one's bearings in thought; and the perceived danger, again, of the *daimon:* I will come back to this possibility of two left (or right) feet at the conclusion of chapter 5.

7. "Postmodernism is the consumption of sheer commodification as a process," Jameson writes. And, for those who have doubts about the *directionality* of dialectical history, its movement from below, from the very low, to above, to the very high, he goes on to say that: "The 'life-style' of the superstate therefore stands in relationship to Marx's 'fetishism' of commodities as the most advanced monotheisms to primitive animisms or the most rudimentary idol worship" (Jameson 1991, x).

8. For a similar reading of Heidegger's politics, see Michael E. Zimmerman (1990), *Heidegger's Confrontation with Modernity: Technology, Politics, and Art.*

9. "*La nature morte*," Derrida ventures, is how one must translate into French the title of Schapiro's essay, "The Still Life." The essay "is a homage rendered, a present made to one dead, a gift dedicated to the memory of Kurt Goldstein" (TP 271), but as Derrida reads Schapiro's essay, it returns what it says (gives) to its sender, and so fits more the logic of commodity-exchange than the logic of the gift.

10. See Hugh Silverman 1994, 140–41 on the *pairing* of Van Gogh's shoes and/ as *gathering.*

11. "A bandaged self-portrait," Derrida suggests in "Restitutions" through his play on the meaning of *bander:* to stretch, to bind, enshroud; also to get an erection. The return-to-self that Derrida analyzes here, particularly in Schapiro's reading, is always an attempted tight attachment; *bander* also implies therefore a finalization— closure, death—of meaning. Such binding is, in every case, a holding onto the inner voice and ear.

12. This matter of *usefulness* in Heidegger involves his putting of *uselessness* to *use*, his (and, in another sense, Derrida's) exploiting of "the surplus value of the out-of-service" (TP 344–45).

13. See Emily Apter's discussion of the intersection of the Marxian and Freudian concepts of fetish in *Feminizing the Fetish* (1991, 1–2).

14. See W. J. T. Mitchell's discussion of *ekphrasis* (giving voice to a mute object) in chapter 5 of *Picture Theory*, "Ekphrasis and the Other." See also Derrida's "The Spatial Arts" interview, particularly his comments on the idea of mutism ("the silence of a thing that can't speak") in painting and discourse.

15. Relevant to this, Simon Firth, in an essay on popular culture, suggests that "high cultural values are by now inextricably entangled with academic practices, rather than with bourgeois consumption" and "the equation of high and academic culture helps to explain why the high/low culture distinction is still so consistently read as a mind/body split" (Firth 1991, 111).

16. The "cutting-out in Schapiro's protocol" leads to "a certain number of simplifications, not to call them anything worse" in his reading of *The Origin of the Work of Art* (TP, 295). This "single stroke" mode of reading Heidegger, and the

politics of the so-called "Heidegger affair," is, it seems to me, always at issue in "Restitutions."

17. Derrida first delivered "Restitutions" on October 6, 1977, at Columbia University, with Schapiro in attendance. See *The Truth in Painting*, 272, on this as "the last act" in a restitution drama.

18. The motif of the path and of walking comes into "Restitutions" through the movement between various senses of the French word for step (walking), *la marche*, which also means margin (border, frame), and which is "just about the 'same' word, the 'same' sense" (TP 264) as *la marque*, mark (imprint, stamp, cipher, signature, sign). Because "speech," for Derrida, is a mark—marked, imprinted, a matter of a "remarkable mode of interlacing" (337)—the "voice" in his text has always already departed from proximity to self; it has, before the beginning, already set out walking. Not unrelated to this is the back-and-forth in "Restitutions" between *la marche, la marque*, and the title word, *pointure*, which can mean "point," "size," "number of [shoes, gloves, etc.]." The word *pointure* is also defined on the first page of Derrida's essay, deriving from the Latin *punctura*, as: a "[t]erm in printing, small iron blade with a point, used to fix the page to be printed on to the tympan. The hole which it makes in the paper. Term in shoemaking, glovemaking: number of stitches in a shoe or glove" [255]).

19. Significantly, the interlace is, historically, a major form of ornament. See Ulmer 1985, 42.

20. Consider, with reference to the "indeterminacy" at issue in Derrida's reading of the painting and its titles, some elements of indeterminacy in his own title, "Restitutions of the truth in pointing [*pointure*]."

21. What is the sex of attachment? "To which sex are the shoes due?" (TP 306). Although neither gives the question thematic attention, there is, in both Schapiro and Heidegger, a "[g]raft of sex onto the shoes" (306), Derrida maintains. See Derrida's discussion of this in "Restitutions" (TP 305–309).

22. "The voice separates," Derrida suggests in the "Spatial Arts" interview; "it is a differential vibration that at the same time interrupts, hinders, prevents access, maintains a distance" (SA 23), and thus in its spacing, allows for someone other than *me* to hear, calls for *you* to respond. The disparateness, or if you like unpairedness, of this "voice," of speaking or writing that is never fully present to itself, gives rise, Derrida says, "in its very detachment, in its dereliction or its separation, to a sort of abyssal surplus value. To a bottomless outbidding" (TP 345). The surplus cannot be captured. We are up against the impossibility of finally "saying" it, even when it comes to old shoes—or for that matter to bottles, cowrie shells, paint brushes, pots, bowls, baskets of vegetables, birds nests, sacks, jars, potatoes, autumn leaves, onions, copper kettles, scabiosa, yellow straw hats, and whatever else van Gogh took up in his continuing Still Life paintings. A bottomless outbidding: the impossibility of framing is what makes this genre of painting a series, repetition without closure, unfinished and unfinishable, *still life*. A bottomless outbidding: the movement this involves would undercut "the ambiguity of the Heideggerian [and Derridean] situation with respect to the metaphysics of presence and logocentrism" (OG 22), the ambiguity with which I am uneasy at the close of chapter 4 and in the following, final, section of chapter 5.

23. David Farrell Krell explains that "[i]n German, *der Riss* is a crack, tear, laceration, cleft, or rift; but it is also a plan or design in drawing. The verb *reissen* from which it derives is cognate with the English word *writing*. *Der Riss* is incised or inscribed as a rune or a letter. Heidegger here employs a series of words (*Abriss, Aufriss, Umriss,* and especially *Grundriss*) to suggest that the rift of world and earth releases a sketch, outline, profile, blueprint, or ground plan. The rift is writ)" (Editor's note in Heidegger 1977, 188). A related issue here is the Heideggerian sense of "frame" and "enframing" (*Gestell*), and not as enclosure and disclosure of truth for a subject. See Heidegger's own comments on this in his suppelement to *The Origin of the Work of Art*; see also Michel Haar's careful discussion of *Gestell* in *The Song of the Earth* (1993).

24. I am reminded here of Derrida's statement in *Limited INC* that "Blinking is a rhythm essential to the mark" (52).

CHAPTER SIX. ARCHITECTURE'S (THE UNIVERSITY'S) *CHORA*: TWO POSTMODERN COLLABORATIONS

1. This sentence would be written, not spoken. As I note in this chapter, Ricoeur argues, in somewhat the same way as do Donald Lowe and Walter Ong, that in spoken dialogue, interpretation is not an issue, for the speech act situation "directly connects the voice of one to the hearing of the other" (Ricoeur 1981, 146–47), confining meaning to an immediate context and to an addressor's intentionality, made evident to an addressee. As I suggest earlier in the book, hearing is never immediate, and speech, as embodied, is always imprinted or "written."

2. *Meta*, over + *pherein*, to carry: movement, navigation, is always at issue in both Ricoeur's and Derrida's work on metaphor (see the transportation icons that open Derrida's "The *Retrait* of Metaphor"), as is the matter of directionality or orientation. For both, although in different ways, the question of orientation is an issue of the architecture of institution.

3. Ricoeur's discussion of structuralism, poststructuralism, and deconstruction consistently associates these developments with death, with "necrologies" that fail to approach the text in its "living totality." These approaches, insofar as they do not think metaphor as meaning, "kill" the text and turn textual analysis into an "operat[ion] on a cadaver." See for example, Ricoeur 1991, 444.

4. "The notion of trope taken as a single word not only snuffs out the potential meaning contained in the admirable initial definition of metaphor; it also breaks up the unity of the problematic of the analogy between ideas, which is thereby dispersed among all the classes of figures" (Ricoeur 1977, 59).

5. Ricoeur's "continuist assimilation or setting into filiation" of Heidegger and Derrida "surprised me," Derrida writes in "The *Retrait* of Metaphor" (RM 13), "as if I had attempted no more than an extension or a *continuous* radicalization of the Heideggerian movement," and "as if I had only generalized what Ricoeur calls Heidegger's 'limited criticism' and as if I had stretched it inordinately, beyond all bounds," and as if Derrida had not "marked, in my Note on Heidegger, a clear and unequivocal reservation; a reservation which, at least in letter, even resembles that

of Ricoeur" on the supposed collusion of the visible/invisible, sensible/intelligible couple (13). Ricoeur's "*continuist presupposition*" (MP 215) also informs his argument that metaphor, properly theorized, works as ongoing semantic gain, and that the history of metaphor went wrong when it started working in the opposite direction.

6. Ricoeur reads Derrida's essay "White Mythology" as an attempt to expose dead metaphors that are lurking everywhere in the philosophical text, to unmask the "*unthought* conjunction of *hidden* metaphysics and *worn-out* metaphor" (Ricoeur 1977, 285), although Derrida, in his response to Ricoeur, says this is "the assertion which I am precisely putting into question" (RM 13). Starting from the "*Exergue*" that constitutes a *parergon* or *ex-ergon*, an outside that belongs inside, the essay "White Mythology," as I read it, examines two articulations of the "metaphor of (the) *usure* (of metaphor)" (MP 210), both of which are found in *The Garden of Epicurus* by Anatole France. In a short section of that book, "Aristos and Polyphilos on the Language of Metaphysics," two interlocutors exchange views on the way in which the metaphysical concept shelters a sensory image, to the point where the image is used up or lost. It's as if metaphysicians were "knife-grinders" who, Polyphilos says, put words, like "medals and coins to the grindstone, to efface the lettering, date and type" until "nothing is visible in their crown-pieces, neither King Edward, the Emperor William, nor the Republic" (France 1926, 194), until not even the coin's exergue remains. Without pronouncing the word itself, Polyphilos articulates here the sense of *usure* as an "erasure by rubbing, exhaustion, crumbling away" (MP 210) of sensory figures by philosophical language, "the erasure of the efficacity of the sensory figure and the *usure* of its effigy" (210), Derrida says. In making this claim, Polyphilos supposes that "a purity of sensory language could have been in circulation at the origin of language" (210), Derrida suggests, and that the *etymon*, the hidden figure, might be restored: "The rest of the dialogue confirms this: it examines, precisely, the possibility of restoring or reactivating, beneath the metaphor which simultaneously hides and is hidden, the 'original figure' of the coin which has been worn away (*usé*), effaced, and polished in the circulation of the philosophical concept" (211). Which leads to Polyphilos's second articulation of the *usure* of metaphor, the sense of *usure* as usury, as that which returns an exhorbitant interest, "the supplementary product of a capital, the exchange which far from losing the original investment would fructify its initial wealth, would increase its return in the form of revenue, additional interest, linguistic surplus value, the two histories of the word remaining indistinguishable" (210). For just as "chemists have reagents whereby they can make the effaced writing of a papyrus or a parchment visible again" (France 1926, 202) so, Polyphilos says, an analogous process of etymological reactivation could work to renew figurative language, "to give back form and colour, to restore the original life and force" (202) to the sensory palimpsest that lurks beneath metaphysics. Derrida positions this exchange on the rubbing away-restoring of the figurative exergue as the *ex-ergon* to his essay, not in order to propound Polyphilos's assertion of a collusion between dead metaphor and metaphysics, as Ricoeur's reading of "White Mythology" suggests, but in order to put that very assertion into question.

7. "The effectiveness of dead metaphor can be inflated," Ricoeur says in his critique of Derrida, "only in semiotic conceptions that impose the primacy of denomination and hence of substitution of meaning" (Ricoeur 1977, 290). And as

Ricoeur argues several times in his book, substitution theory condemns metaphor to ornamentation, to no more than pleasing adornment, "for if the metaphorical term is really a substituted term, it carries no new information, since the absent term (if one exists) can be brought in; and if there is no information conveyed, then metaphor has only an ornamental, decorative value" (20). For Ricoeur, of course, there is no such thing as a dead metaphor, which means that there are no metaphors to be found in dictionaries.

8. I have not taken up Ricoeur's referencing of Gadamer in *The Rule of Metaphor*, though his relation to Gadamer, and to Hegel, is certainly relevant to my study. I could draw as well on the so-called Derrida-Gadamer debate, especially where the question of the signature is concerned. On this, see Derrida's "Interpreting Signatures."

9. Derrida's essay first appeared in French under the title "*Chôra*" in *Poikilia: Études Offertes À Jean-Pierre Vernant*, Centre de Recherches Comparées Sur Les Sociétés Anciennes, Paris: Les Éditions de l'École des Hautes Études en Sciences Sociales, 1987: 265–96. An English translation by Ian McLeod, "*Khora*," is included in Derrida's *On The Name* (Stanford University Press, 1995: 87–127). I am following the translation that appears in Derrida and Eisenman, *Chora L Works*, 15–32, the volume, edited by Jeffrey Kipnis and Thomas Lesser, that documents the Derrida-Eisenman collaboration and that includes, along with drawings of the project, correspondence, and transcripts of meetings that took place during their collaboration, Derrida's essay "Why Peter Eisenman Writes Such Good Books," Eisenman's "Separate Tricks," and Kipnis's "Twisting the Separatrix." My references to "*Chora*" and to "Why Peter Eisenman Writes Such Good Books" are cited by page numbers from this volume (abbreviated as CW). My references to Kipnis are taken from the shorter version of "Twisting the Separatrix," which is published as "The law of ana-" in *Recente Projecten Peter Eisenman Recent Projects*, edited by Arie Graafland (listed in Works Cited as Kipnis 1989).

10. The translators of "The *Retrait* of Metaphor" offer this prefatory note on the title word: "The word *retrait* has a variety of meanings in French: withdrawal (in monetary and military senses), retrace (the going back over again, re-tracing, re-marking of something), recess (as in architecture), and retraction. *Retrait*, by metonymy, also touches on: *retraite*: retreat, retirement, place of retirement, shelter or refuge; *trait*: line, mark, stroke, or feature; *traite*: road, place of passage, bank draft or bill or exchange; *retirer*: to retreat, to withdraw (again, in monetary and military senses), to reprint, and *se retirer*: to retire, to retreat. *Retrait* thus opens up the strategic relationships, which Derrida discusses in this text, between metaphor, withdrawals, retreats, economy, the pathway, passage, and circulation. (The phonic and graphic interplay of *rt-tr* in Derrida's French has been signalled by preserving *retrait* and *trait* as often as possible in the translation" (RM 4).

11. This is Derrida's problem with Ricoeur's account of *living* metaphor as semantic production, also with Ricoeur's critique of "deconstruction" as supposedly working in the opposite direction, to effect the progressive wearing-out of meaning by its unveiling of metaphors that are already *dead*: whether the account of metaphor concerns *usure* as the "continuous and linearly accumulative capitalization" (RM 13) of semantic surplus (*plus-value*), or whether it concerns *usure* in the opposite sense of

regular semantic loss, continuous wear and tear of the concept, a structure, Derrida says, is not brought into the account.

12. "What is hiding under this uncanny park that somehow claims to be the official park of the Uncanny? Or really, what would a labyrinth be without a minotaur: a labyrinth without blood?" (Hollier 1992, xi). See Hollier's discussion of la Villette, particularly in relation to Bataille's "Abattoir" and "Architecture" essays. "The greatest motive for Bataille's aggressivity toward architecture is its anthropomorphism" (xi).

13. No account of metaphor can fail to deal with the issue of animality that Derrida takes up in "White Mythology," the issue of animality that is bound up with Aristotle's founding metaphorics and that Ricoeur, in his theory of metaphor-as-meaning, leaves out. See Derrida's analysis of this issue (MP 235–38), where Aristotle's elaboration of the difference between animals and man is shown to depend on man's capacity for phonetic signification.

14. For Derrida, no pure philosophy of *chora* is possible; no logocentric account of *chora* or indeed of the "philosophy of Plato" could but "misrecognize or violently deny" (CW 27) the *ana-logical* structure of the *Timaeus*. "Platonism," and indeed the whole history of philosophy based on it, is more than a thetic abstraction, an ontology or dialectic, Derrida says. It is also "a certain disorder, some potential incoherence, and some heterogeneity in the organization of the theses" (28).

15. For Hegel, Derrida notes, "[i]n a philosophical text, the function of myth is at times a sign of philosophical impotence, the incapacity to accede to the concept as such and to keep to it, at other times the index of a dialectic and above all didactic potency, the pedagogic mastery of the serious philosopher in full possession of the philosopheme. Simultaneously or successively, Hegel seems to recognize in Plato both the impotence and this mastery" (CW 20).

16. In connection with Plato's *triton genos*, consider the three "steps," "stages," or "signs" that Derrida works through in "How To Avoid Speaking: Denials," that he says are "essentially alien to dialectic," and that "do not form the moments or signs of a history. They will not disclose the order of a teleology" (HAS 30). See also Derrida's reference to the "three sites" of *Choral L Work* in "Why Peter Eisenman Writes Such Good Books" (CW 95–101).

17. *Shaking*, "in the sense that *sollicitare*, in old Latin, means to shake as a whole, to make tremble in entirety" (MP 21), is a spacing out, as I have already suggested. It entails, as Derrida notes in *Positions*, a movement of setting aside, of setting self (presence) aside: "It marks what is set aside from itself, what interrupts every self-identity, every punctual assemblage of the self, every self-homogeneity, self-interiority" (P 106–107).

18. In Hebrew, *chora* means to rend, tear, which relates to the ritual tearing of a garment worn by the mourner at a Jewish funeral after the eulogy. The ritual dates back to Jacob, who tore his garment on learning of the death of Joseph (Samuel 21: 17–27). King David did the same when he heard of the tragic death of his friend Jonathan. In *Revolution In Poetic Language* (as discussed in Graafland 1989, 113), Kristeva refers to *chora*'s rending of the thetic surface. This tearing would be a going-out, what Tschumi calls a "dis-integration" (Tschumi 1987, vii): not a destruction, but on the contrary, a precondition of survival. See Graafland (1989, 107; 111–12).

WORKS CITED

1. WORKS BY JACQUES DERRIDA

———. 1973. *Speech and Phenomena: And Other Essays on Husserl's Theory of Signs.* Translated by David B. Allison. Evanston: Northwestern University Press.

———. 1974. *Of Grammatology.* Translated by Gayatri Spivak. Baltimore: Johns Hopkins University Press.

———. 1977. *Limited INC.* Translated by Samuel Weber. Baltimore: Johns Hopkins University Press.

———. 1978. "The *Retrait* of Metaphor." Translated by the editors. *Enclitic* 2: 4–33.

———. 1978. *Writing and Difference.* Translated by Alan Bass. Chicago: University of Chicago Press.

———. 1979. "Living On: Border-lines." In *Deconstruction and Criticism.* Translated by J. Hulbert. Edited by Harold Bloom et al. New York: Seabury, 75–176.

———. 1981. *Positions.* Translated by Alan Bass. Chicago: University of Chicago Press.

———. 1982. *Margins of Philosophy.* Translated by Alan Bass. Chicago: University of Chicago Press.

———. 1982. "Of An Apocalyptic Tone Recently Adopted in Philosophy." Translated by John P. Leavey Jr. *Semeia* 23: 63–97.

———. 1983. "*Geschlecht*: sexual difference, ontological difference." *Research In Phenomenology* 13: 65–83.

———. 1983. "The Principle of Reason: The University in the Eyes of its Pupils." Translated by Catherine Porter and Edward P. Morris. *Diacritics* (Fall): 3–20.

———. 1984. "Languages and Institutions of Philosophy." Translated by Sylvia Söderlind, Rebecca Comay, Barbara Havercroft, Joseph Adamson. *RS/SI* 4, 2: 91–154.

———. 1984. "Deconstruction and the Other: An Interview with Richard Kearney." In Richard Kearney, *Dialogues with Contemporary Continental Thinkers.* Oxford: Manchester University Press, 107–26.

———. 1985. *The Ear of the Other: Otobiography, Transference, Translation.* Translated by Peggy Kamuf. Edited by Christie McDonald. New York: Schocken.

————. 1986. *Glas*. Translated by John P. Leavey Jr. and Richard Rand. Lincoln: University of Nebraska Press.

————. 1986. "Jacques Derrida on the University." Interview by Imre Salusinszky. *Southern Review* 19, 1 (March): 3–12.

————. 1986. "*Point de folie: Maintenant l'architecture*." Translated by Kate Linker. *AA Files* 12: 65–75.

————. 1986. "The Age of Hegel." Translated by Susan Winnett. In *Demarcating the Disciplines: Philosophy, Literature, Art*. Edited by Samuel Weber. Minneapolis: University of Minnesota Press, 3–45.

————. 1987. "*Geschlecht* II: Heidegger's Hand." Translated by John P. Leavey Jr. In *Deconstruction and Philosophy: The Texts of Jacques Derrida*. Edited by John Sallis. Chicago: University of Chicago Press, 161–96.

————. 1987. "*Chôra*." In *Poikilia: Études Offertes À Jean-Pierre Vernant*. Centre de Recherches Comparées Sur Les Sociétés Anciennes. Paris: Les Éditions de l'École des Hautes Études en Sciences Sociales, 265–96.

————. 1987. *The Truth In Painting*. Translated by Geoff Bennington and Ian McLeod. Chicago: University of Chicago Press.

————. 1989. "How to Avoid Speaking: Denials." Translated by Ken Frieden. In *Languages of the Unsayable: The Play of Negativity in Literature and Literary Theory*. Edited by Sanford Budick and Wolfgang Iser. New York: Columbia University Press, 3–70.

————. 1989. *Of Spirit: Heidegger and the Question*. Translated by Geoffrey Bennington and Rachel Bowlby. Chicago and London: University of Chicago Press.

————. 1989. "Interpreting Signatures (Nietzsche/Heidegger): Two Questions." Translated by Diane Michelfelder and Richard Palmer. In *Dialogue and Deconstruction: The Gadamer-Derrida Encounter*. Edited by Diane Michelfelder and Richard Palmer. Albany: State University of New York Press, 58–71.

————. 1989. "On Colleges and Philosophy." Interview by Geoff Bennington. In *Postmodernism: ICA Documents*. Edited by Lisa Appignanesi. London: Free Association, 209–28.

————. 1991. *Cinders*. Translated by Ned Lukacher. Lincoln: University of Nebraska Press.

————. 1991. "'Eating Well,' or the Calculation of the Subject: An Interview with Jacques Derrida." Translated by Peter Connor and Avital Ronnell. In *Who Comes after the Subject?* Edited by Eduardo Cadava, Peter Connor, Jean-Luc Nancy. New York: Routledge, 96–119.

————. 1992. "*Mochlos*; or, The Conflict of the Faculties." Translated by Richard Rand and Amy Wygant. In *Logomachia: The Conflict of the Faculties*. Edited by Richard Rand. Lincoln: University of Nebraska Press, 3–34.

————. 1992. "Canons and Metonymies." Interview by Richard Rand. In *Logomachia: The Conflict of the Faculties*. Edited by Richard Rand. Lincoln: University of Nebraska Press, 197–218.

————. 1992. *The Other Heading: Reflections on Today's Europe*. Translated by Pascale-Anne Brault and Michael Naas. Bloomingtion: Indiana University Press.

————. 1992. *Points . . . Interviews 1974–1994*. Edited by Elisabeth Weber. Translated by Peggy Kamuf and others. Stanford: Stanford University Press.

————. 1992. "Before the Law." Translated by Avital Ronell and Christine Roulston. In *Jacques Derrida: Acts of Literature*. Edited by Derek Attridge. New York: Routledge, 181–220.

————. 1993. "Heidegger's Ear: Philopolemology (*Geschlecht* IV)." Translated by John P. Leavey Jr. In *Reading Heidegger: Commemorations*. Edited by John Sallis. Bloomington: Indiana University Press, 163–218.

————. 1993. *Memoirs of the Blind: The Self-Portrait and Other Ruins*. Translated by Pascale-Anne Brault and Michael Naas. Chicago: The University of Chicago Press.

————. 1994. "The Spatial Arts: An Interview with Jacques Derrida." By Peter Brunette and David Wills. In *Deconstruction and the Visual Arts: Art, Media, Architecture*. Edited by Peter Brunette and David Wills. Cambridge, Mass.: Cambridge University Press, 9–32.

————. 1994. *Specters of Marx: The State of the Debt, the Work of Mourning, and the New International*. Translated by Peggy Kamuf. New York: Routledge.

————. 1995. "*Khora*." Translated by Ian McLeod. In Jacques Derrida, *On The Name*. Translated by David Wood, John P. Leavey Jr., Ian McLeod. Edited by Thomas Dutoit. Stanford: Stanford University Press, 87–127.

————. 1995. *The Gift of Death*. Translated by David Wills. Chicago: University of Chicago Press.

————. 1996. *Resistances of Psychoanalysis*. Translated by Peggy Kamuf, Pascale-Anne Brault, Michael Naas. Stanford: Stanford University Press.

————. 2000. *Of Hospitality: Anne Dufourmantelle Invites Jacques Derrida to Respond*. Translated by Rachel Bowlby. Stanford: Stanford University Press.

————. 2001. "The Future of the Profession or the Unconditional University." Translated by Peggy Kamuf. In *Derrida Downunder*. Edited by Laurence Simmons and Heather Worth. Palmerston North, New Zealand: Dunmore Press, 233–47.

————. 2002. *Who's Afraid of Philosophy? Right to Philosophy I*. Translated by Jan Plug. Stanford: Stanford University Press.

Derrida, Jacques, and Peter Eisenman. 1997. *Chora L Works*. Edited by Jeffrey Kipnis and Thomas Leeser. New York: The Monacelli Press.

2. OTHER SOURCES

Abraham, Nicolas, and Maria Torok. 1987. "Mourning or Melancholia: Introjection versus Incorporation." In *The Shell and the Kernel*, Volume I. Edited and translated by Nicholas Rand. Chicago: University of Chicago Press, 125–38.

Apter, Emily. 1991. *Feminizing the Fetish: Psychoanalysis and Narrative Obsession in Turn-of-the-Century France*. Ithaca: Cornell University Press.

Aristotle. 1984. "History of Animals." In *The Complete Works of Aristotle*. The Revised Oxford Translation. Volume I. Edited by Jonathan Barnes. Princeton: Princeton University Press, 774–993.

Bahti, Timothy. 1992. "The Injured University." In *Logomachia: The Conflict of the Faculties*. Edited by Richard Rand. Lincoln: University of Nebraska Press, 59–76.

Bal, Mieke. 1991. *Reading "Rembrandt": Beyond the Word-Image Opposition.* Cambridge: Cambridge University Press.

———. 1996. *Double Exposures: The Subject of Cultural Analysis.* New York: Routledge.

Baudrillard, Jean. 1987. "Préface." In Bernard Tschumi, *Parc-Ville Villette.* Paris: Champ Vallon, 4–5.

Bédard, Jean-François. 1994. "Introduction." In *Cities of Artificial Excavation: The Work Of Peter Eisenman, 1978–1988.* Edited by Jean-François Bédard. Montréal: Centre Canadien d'Architecture/Canadian Centre for Architecture, 9–18.

Beistegui, Miguel de. 1998. *Heidegger & the Political: Dystopias.* London: Routledge.

Bercuson, David J., Robert Bothwell, and J. L. Granastein. 1984. *The Great Brain Robbery: Canada's Universities on the Road to Ruin.* Toronto: McClelland and Stewart.

Boles, Daralice. 1987. "The Point of No Return." *Progressive Architecture* 68 : 94–97.

Bronfen, Elisabeth. 1992. *Over Her Dead Body: Death, Femininity, and the Aesthetic.* New York: Routledge.

Dallery, Arleen, B., Charles E. Scott, and P. Holley Roberts. 1992. *Ethics and Danger: Essays on Heidegger and Continental Thought.* Albany: State University of New York Press.

Davis, Lennard J. 1995. *Enforcing Normalcy: Disability, Deafness, and the Body.* London, New York: Verso.

Descartes, René. 1985. *Optics.* Translated by John Cottingham, Robert Stoothoff, Dugald Murdoch. In *The Philosophical Writings of Descartes.* Vol. 1. Cambridge: Cambridge University Press, 152–75.

Dunn, Leslie C., and Nancy A. Jones, eds. 1994. *Embodied Voices: Representing Female Vocality in Western Culture.* Cambridge: Cambridge University Press.

Dutoit, Thomas. 1995. "Translating the Name?" In Jacques Derrida, *On The Name.* Translated by David Wood, John P. Leavey Jr., Ian McLeod. Stanford: Stanford University Press, ix–xvi.

Eisenman, Peter. 1994. *Cities of Artificial Excavation: The Work of Peter Eisenman, 1978–1988.* Edited by Jean-François Bédard. Montréal: Rizzoli.

———. 1995. *Eisenman Architects: Selected and Current Works.* Mulgrave, Australia: The Image Publishing Group.

Enterline, Lynn. 2000. *The Rhetoric of the Body: From Ovid to Shakespeare.* Cambridge: Cambridge University Press.

Farías, Victor. 1989. *Heidegger and Nazism.* Translated by Paul Burrell and Gabriel R. Ricci. Philadelphia: Temple University Press.

Fenves, Peter, ed. 1993. *Raising the Tone of Philosophy: Late Essays by Immanuel Kant, Transformative Critique by Jacques Derrida.* Baltimore: The Johns Hopkins University Press.

Firth, Simon. 1991. "The Good, the Bad, and the Indifferent: Defending Popular Culture from the Populists." *Diacritics* 21, 4 (Winter): 102–15.

Foster, Hal, ed. 1988. "Preface." In *Vision and Visuality.* Edited by Hal Foster. Seattle: Bay Press, ix–xiv.

Foucault, Michel. 1965. *Madness and Civilization.* Translated by Richard Howard. New York: Random House.

France, Anatole. 1926. *The Garden of Epicurus.* Translated by Alfred Allinson. New York: Dodd, Mead and Co.

Freud, Sigmund. 1953. "Medusa's Head" (1940). Translated by James Strachey. In *The Standard Edition of the Complete Psychological Works of Sigmund Freud*, Volume VII. London: Hogarth Press, 273–74.

———. 1961. "Fetishism" (1927). Translated by James Strachey. In *The Standard Edition of the Complete Psychological Works of Sigmund Freud*, Volume XXI.London: Hogarth Press, 152–57.

———. 1984. "Mourning and Melancholia" (1917). Translated by James Strachey. In *On Metapsychology*. The Penguin Freud Library, Volume 11. Harmondsworth: Penguin, 251–68.

———. 1985. "The 'Uncanny'" (1919). Translated by James Strachey. In *Sigmund Freud: Art and Literature*. The Penguin Freud Library, Volume 14. New York: Penguin, 335–76.

Gilmour, John C. 1988. *"The Truth In Painting."* A Review. *The Journal of Aesthetics and Art Criticism* 46: 519–21.

Graafland, Arie, ed. 1989. *Recente projecten Peter Eisenman Recent projects*. Nijmegen: SUN.

Greene, Theodore M. 1980. "Introduction: The Historical Context and Religious Significance of Kant's *Religion*." In Immanuel Kant, *Religion Within the Limits of Reason Alone*. Translated by Theodore M. Greene and Hoyt H. Hudson. New York: Harper, ix–lxxviii.

Haar, Michel. 1993. *The Song of the Earth: Heidegger and the Grounds of the History of Being*. Trans. Reginald Lilly. Bloomington: Indiana University Press.

Hartman, Geoffrey H. 1975. "Monsieur Texte: On Jacques Derrida, His *Glas*." *Georgia Review* 29: 759–798.

Hegel, G. W. F. 1970. *Philosophy of Nature. Being Part Two of the Encyclopedia of The Philosophical Sciences (1830) Translated from Nicolin and Pöggeler's Edition (1959) and from the Zusatz in Michelet's Text (1847)*. Translated by A. V. Miller. Oxford: Clarendon Press.

———. 1975. *Aesthetics: Lectures on Fine Art*. Volumes I and II. Translated by T. M. Knox Oxford: Clarendon Press.

———. 1977. *Phenomenology of Spirit*. Translated by A. V. Miller. Oxford: Oxford University Press.

———. 1984. *Hegel: The Letters*. Translated by Clark Butler and Christiane Seiler with commentary by Clark Butler. Bloomington: Indiana University Press.

———. 1988. *Lectures on the Philosophy of Religion*. Translated by R. F. Brown, P. C. Hodgson, J. M. Stewart, with the assistance of H. S. Harris. Edited by Peter C. Hodgson. Berkeley: University of California Press.

———. 1991a. *The Philosophy of History*. Translated by J. Sibree. Buffalo: Prometheus Books.

——— 1991b. *Elements of the Philosophy of Right*. Translated by H. B. Nisbet. Edited by Allen W. Wood. Cambridge: Cambridge University Press.

Heidegger, Martin. 1958a. *What Is Philosophy?* Translated by William Kluback and Jean T. Wilde. New York: Twayne Publishers.

———. 1958b. *The Question of Being*. Translated byWilliam Kluback and Jean T. Wilde. New York: Twayne Publishers.

———. 1959. *An Introduction to Metaphysics*. Translated by Ralph Manheim. New Haven: Yale University Press.

———. 1962. *Being and Time*. Translated by John Macquarrie and Edward Robinson. New York: Harper and Row.

———. 1968. *What Is Called Thinking?* Translated by G. Glenn Gray. New York: Harper and Row.

———. 1971. *On the Way to Language*. Translated by Peter D. Hertz. New York: Harper and Row.

———. 1977a. *The Origin of the Work of Art*. In *Basic Writings*. Edited and translated by David Farrell Krell. San Francisco: Harper, 138–212.

———. 1977b. *The Question Concerning Technology and Other Essays*. Translated by William Lovitt. New York: Harper and Row.

———. 1984. *The Metaphysical Foundations of Logic*. Translated by Michael Heim. Bloomington: Indiana University Press.

———. 1985. "The Self-Assertion of the German University and The Rectorate 1933/34: Facts and Thoughts." Translated by Karsten Haries. *Review of Metaphysics* 38 (March): 467–502.

———. 1991. *The Principle of Reason* (*Der Satz vom Grund*). Translated by Reginald Lilly. Bloomington: Indiana University Press.

———. 1992. *Paramenides*. Translated by André Schuwer and Richard Rojcewicz. Bloomington: Indiana University Press.

———. 1995. *The Fundamental Concepts of Metaphysics: World, Finitude, Solitude*. Translated by William McNeil and Nicholas Walker. Bloomington: Indiana University Press.

Hollier, Denis. 1992. *Against Architecture: The Writings of Georges Bataille*. Cambridge: MIT Press.

Jameson, Fredric. 1982. "Interview." *Diacritics* 12, 3 (Fall): 72–91.

———. 1988. "Periodizing the 60s." In *The Ideologies of Theory, Volume Two: Syntax of History*. Minneapolis: University of Minnesota Press, 178–208.

———. 1991. *Postmodernism or, the Cultural Logic of Late Capitalism*. Durham: Duke University Press.

Jay, Martin. 1988. "Scopic Regimes of Modernity." In *Vision and Visuality*. Edited by Hal Foster. Seattle: Bay Press, 2–27.

———. 1994. *Downcast Eyes: the Denigration of Vision in Twentieth-Century French Thought*. Berkeley: University of California Press.

Juers, Evelyn. 2000. "She Wanders: An Essay in Gothic." *Heat* 15: 25–44.

Kant, Immanuel. 1952. *The Critique of Judgement*. Translated by James Creed Meredith. Oxford: Clarendon.

———. 1958. "Von einem neuerdings erhobenen vornehmen Ton in der Philosophie." *Schriften zur Metaphysik und Logik*, vol. 3, 377–97. Wiesbaden: Insel-Verlag. See also: "On A Newly Arisen Superior Tone in Philosophy." Translated by Peter Fenves. In *Raising The Tone of Philosophy: Late Essays by Immanuel Kant, Transformative Critique by Jacques Derrida*. Edited by Peter Fenves. Baltimore: Johns Hopkins University Press, 1993, 51–81.

———. 1960. *Religion Within the Limits of Reason Alone*. Translated by Theodore M. Greene and Hoyt H. Hudson. New York: Harper.

———. 1966. *Critique of Pure Reason*. Translated by F. Max Müller. New York: Anchor.

———. 1970. "What is Orientation in Thinking?" In *Kant: Political Writings*. Edited by Hans Reiss. Translated by H. B. Nisbet. Cambridge: Cambridge University Press, 237–99.

———. 1974. *Anthropology From A Pragmatic Point of View*. Translated by Mary J. Gregor. The Hague: Martinus Nijhoff.

——— 1979. *The Conflict of the Faculties*. Translated by Mary J. Gregor. Lincoln: University of Nebraska Press.

Kipnis, Jeffrey. 1989. "The Law of Ana—On Choral Works." In *Recente projecten Peter Eisenman Recent projects*. Edited by Arie Graafland. Nijmegen: SUN, 145–60.

Krell, David Farrell. 1992a. *Daimon Life: Heidegger and Life-Philosophy*. Bloomington: Indiana University Press.

———. 1992b. "Of Spirit and the *Daimon*: On Derrida's *De l'esprit*." In *Ethics and Danger: Essays on Heidegger and Continental Thought*. Edited by Arleen Dallery and Charles Scott with P. Holley Roberts. Albany: State University of New York Press, 59–70.

———. 1993. "Spiriting Heidegger." In *Of Derrida, Heidegger, and Spirit*. Edited by David Wood. Evanston: Northwestern University Press, 11–40.

———. 2000. *The Purest of Bastards: Works of Mourning, Art, and Affirmation in the Thought of Jacques Derrida*. University Park: The Pennsylvania State University Press.

Kristeva, Julia. 1974. *Revolution in Poetic Language*. Translated by Leon Roudiez. New York: Columbia University Press.

———. 1980. *Desire in Language*. Translated by Leon Roudiez. New York: Columbia University Press.

———. 1989. *Black Sun: Depression and Melancholy*. Translated by Leon Roudiez. New York: Columbia University Press.

Lacoue-Labarthe, Philippe. 1990. *Heidegger, Art, and Politics: The Fiction of the Political*. Translated by Chris Turner. London: Blackwell.

Lang, Berel. 1996. *Heidegger's Silence*. Ithaca: Cornell University Press.

Latimer, Dan. 1984. "Jameson and Post-Modernism." *New Left Review* 148: 116–28.

Lawlor, Leonard. 1983. "Event and Repeatability: Ricoeur and Derrida in Debate." *PPRE/TEXT* 4, 3–4: 317–34.

Leavey, John, P., Jr. 1986. "This (then) will not have been a book . . ." In John P. Leavey Jr., *Glassary*. Lincoln: University of Nebraska Press, 22–128.

Lowe, Donald, M. 1982. *History of Bourgeois Perception*. Chicago: University of Chicago Press.

Lukacher, Ned. 1991. "Introduction: Mourning Becomes Telepathy." In Jacques Derrida, *Cinders*. Translated by Ned Lukacher. Lincoln: University of Nebraska Press, 1–18.

Lyotard, Jean-François. 1988. *The Differend: Phrases in Dispute*. Translated by Georges van den Abbeele. Minneapolis: University of Minnesota Press.

———. 1990. *Heidegger and "the Jews."* Translated by Andreas Michel and Mark Roberts. Minneapolis: University of Minnesota Press.

McCance, Dawne. 1996. *Posts: Re Addressing the Ethical*. Albany: State University of New York Press.

Mitchell, W. J. T. 1994. *Picture Theory*. Chicago: University of Chicago Press.

Mulvey, Laura. 1996. *Fetishism and Curiosity*. Bloomington: Indiana University Press.

Newman, John Henry Cardinal. 1959. *The Idea of a University*. New York: Image.

Oliver, Kelly. 1997. *Family Values: Subjects Between Nature and Culture*. New York: Routledge.

Olkowski, Dorothea. 1985. "If the Shoe Fits: Derrida and the Orientation of Thought." In *Hermeneutics and Deconstruction*. Edited by Hugh J. Silverman and Don Ihde. Albany: State University of New York Press, 262–69.

O'Malley, C. D. 1964. *Andreas Vesalius of Brussels 1514–1564*. Berkeley and Los Angeles: University of California Press.

Ong, Walter, J. 1982. *Orality and Literacy: The Technologizing of the Word*. London: Methuen.

Ovid. *Metamorphoses*. 1986. Translated by A. D. Melville. Oxford: Oxford University Press.

Panofsky. Erwin.1991. *Perspective as Symbolic Form*. New York: Zone Books.

Papadakis, Andreas, Catherine Cooke, and Andrew Benjamin, eds., 1989. *Deconstruction: Omnibus Volume*. New York: Rizzoli.

Pelikan, Jaroslav. 1992. *The Idea of a University: A Reexamination*. New Haven: Yale University Press.

Pérez-Gómez, Alberto. 1994. "*Chora*: the Space of Architectural Representation." In *Chora 1: Intervals in the Philosophy of Architecture*. Edited by Alberto Pérez-Gómez and Stephen Parcell. Montréal: McGill-Queens, 2–34.

Pinkard, Terry. 2000. *Hegel: A Biography*. Cambridge: Cambridge University Press.

Plato. 1965. *Timaeus and Critias*. Translated by Desmond Lee. London: Penguin.

Rand, Richard. 1992. "Preface." In *Logomachia: The Conflict of the Faculties*. Edited by Richard Rand. Lincoln: University of Nebraska Press, vii–xii.

Rée, Jonathan. 1999. *I See a Voice: Deafness, Language, and the Senses—a Philosophical History*. New York: Metropolitan Books.

Ricoeur, Paul. 1976. *Interpretation Theory*. Fort Worth: Texas Christian University Press.

———. 1977. *The Rule of Metaphor*. Translated by Robert Czerny, with Kathleen McLaughlin and John Costello, S. J. Toronto: University of Toronto Press.

———. 1981. *Hermeneutics and the Human Sciences: Essays on Language, Action, and Interpretation*. Translated and edited by John B. Thompson. Cambridge: Cambridge University Press.

———. 1991. *Reflection and Imagination: A Ricoeur Reader*. Edited by Mario J. Valdés. Toronto: University of Toronto Press.

Rockmore, Tom. 1995. *Heidegger and French Philosophy: Humanism, Antihumanism, and Being*. New York: Routledge.

Russo, Mary. 1994. *The Female Grotesque: Risk, Excess, Modernity*. New York: Routledge.

Sacks, Oliver. 1989. *Seeing Voices: A Journey into the World of the Deaf*. Berkeley: University of California Press.

Saussure, Ferdinand de. 1959. *Course In General Linguistics*. Translated by Wade Baskin. New York: McGraw-Hill.

Sawdy, Jonathan. 1990. "The Fate of Marsyas: Dissecting the Renaissance Body." In *Renaissance Bodies: The Human Figure in English Culture c.1540–1660*. Edited by Lucy Gent and Nigel Llewellyn. London: Reaktion Books, 111–35.

———. 1995. *The Body Emblazoned: Dissection and the Human Body in Renaissance Culture*. New York: Routledge.

Schapiro, Meyer. 1994. "The Still Life as a Personal Object: A Note on Heidegger and Van Gogh." In *The Reach of the Mind*. Edited by M. I. Simmel. New York: Springer Publishing Company, 203–209.

Schelling, F. W. J. 1986. *On University Studies*. Translated by E. S. Morgan. Athens, Ohio: Ohio University Press.

Schmidt, Leigh Eric. 2000. *Hearing Things: Religion, Illusion, and the American Enlightenment*. Cambridge: Harvard University Press.

Segal, Charles. 1994a. "The Gorgon and the Nightingale: The Voice of Female Lament and Pindar's Twelfth *Pythian Ode*." In *Embodied Voices: Representing Female Vocality in Western Culture*. Edited by Leslie C. Dunn and Nancy A. Jones. Cambridge: Cambridge University Press, 17–34.

———. 1994b. *Singers, Heroes, and Gods in the Odyssey*. Ithaca: Cornell University Press,

Silverman, Hugh J. 1994. "The Autobiographical Textuality of Heidegger's Shoes." In *Textualities: Between Hermeneutics and Deconstruction*. New York: Routledge, 134–48.

Smith, Robert. 1995. *Derrida and Autobiography*. Cambridge: Cambridge University Press.

Spengler, Oswald. 1931. *Man and Technics: A Contribution to a Philosophy of Life*. Translated by Charles Francis Atkinson. Westport: Greenwood Press.

Spivak, Gayatri. 1977. "*Glas*-piece: A *Compte Rendu*." *Diacritics*. 7, 3: 22–43.

Spanos, William, V. 1993. *Heidegger and Criticism: Retrieving the Cultural Politics of Destruction*. Minneapolis: University of Minnesota Press.

———. 2000. *America's Shadow: An Anatomy of Empire*. Minneapolis: University of Minnesota Press.

Todd, Jane Marie. 1986. "Autobiography and the Case of the Signature: Reading Derrida's *Glas*." *Comparative Literature* 38, 1: 1–19.

Tschumi, Bernard. 1987. *Cinegram Folie: Le Parc De La Villette*. Paris: Champ Vallon.

———. 1989. "Parc de la Villette." In *Deconstruction: Ommibus Volume*. Edited by Andreas Papadakis, Catherine Cooke, Andrew Benjamin. New York: Rizzoli, 175–83.

———. 1998. *Architecture and Disjunction*. Cambridge: MIT Press.

Tyler, Parker. 1956 "Andy Warhol." *Artnews* 55 (December): 56.

Ulmer, Gregory L. 1985. *Applied Grammatology: Post(e)-Pedagogy from Jacques Derrida to Joseph Beuys*. Baltimore and London: Johns Hopkins University Press.

———. 1986. "Sounding the Unconscious." In John P. Leavey Jr., *Glassary*. Lincoln: University of Nebraska Press, 23–135.

Warhol, Andy. 1971. *Andy Warhol: His Early Works 1947–1959*. Complied by Andreas Brown. New York: Gotham Book Mart Gallery.

———. 1985. *Andy Warhol Prints*. Edited by Frayda Feldman and Jörg Schellemann. New York: Ronald Feldman Fine Art Inc.

Wigley, Mark. 1987. "Postmortem Architecture: The Taste of Derrida." *Perpsecta* 23: 157–72.

———. 1993. *The Architecture of Deconstruction: Derrida's Haunt*. Cambridge: MIT Press.

Wolin, Richard. 1990. *The Politics of Being: The Political Thought of Martin Heidegger.* New York: Columbia University Press.

———. ed. 1993. *The Heidegger Controversy: A Critical Reader.* Cambridge: MIT Press.

Zimmerman, Michael. 1990. *Heidegger's Confrontation with Modernity.* Bloomington: Indiana University Press.

INDEX